TEENAGERS COME AND PRAY!

Celebrating Milestones,
Memorials & Holy Days

MICHAEL D. AUSPERK

XXIII

TWENTY-THIRD PUBLICATIONS
Mystic, CT 06355

Twenty-Third Publications
185 Willow Street
P.O. Box 180
Mystic, CT 06355
(203) 536-2611
800-321-0411

ISBN 0-89622-642-5
Library of Congress Catalog Card Number 94-61851
Printed in the U.S.A.

Acknowledgments

All scriptural quotations are from *The Holy Bible: New Revised Standard Version*, © 1989, Division of Christian Education of the National Council of the Churches of Christ in the United States of America; published by Oxford University Press, New York.

I am indebted to those who assisted me in this project: to the youth group at St. John Neumann Parish in Strongsville, Ohio, the Confirmation Catechists, Facilitators, Core Team Members, and Candidates of St. Joseph Parish, Amherst, Ohio, Rev. Larry Martello, Sr. Jeanette Brown, S.N.D. (for the music suggestions), and to my parents, Dave and Ginny Ausperk, to whom I dedicate the efforts here because they first taught me and my brothers how to pray at home around the dinner table and next to our beds, which helps us now at home and away.

Contents

TEENAGERS COME AND PRAY!

Introduction

In Matthew's gospel (18:19), Jesus instructs his disciples, "If two of you agree on earth about anything you ask, it will be done for you. . . ." Jesus was very clear: If you join together in prayer, God will hear and answer your prayer. He then goes on to say: "Where two or three are gathered in my name, I am there among them." He assured his disciples and future followers that he would be with us whenever we were together in his name or in prayer.

Too often these days we feel abandoned by family, friends, the church, and sometimes by God. Either because of our own attitude, mobile society, or individualization, we often feel alone. Prayer, especially social or communal prayer, is a way to remind ourselves that we are, in fact, not alone or abandoned. We may, indeed, *feel* alone, but as God's children we know from Jesus' promise that we will never be alone, that God will always be with us.

In recent years there has been a strong emphasis on youth ministry and youth groups. Where youth ministry used to mean religious education programs and schools, it now encompasses a wide variety of programs and activities, which include prayer time, service projects, education programs, and social opportunities.

Working with a large group of active high school students at St. John Neumann Parish in Strongsville, Ohio, I wrote a Good Friday mime service for them to present to the parish. They were excited about the presentation and the parish was very receptive. With that encouragement I wrote prayer and mime services for various other occasions; as

presented here, they may be used in a school or parish setting.

With such a mix of words and action we experience with two senses what the disciples experienced completely in the presence of Jesus. Words accompanied with appropriate activity can instill the message of Scripture in us more deeply than just reading and listening can. Also, joining movement and sight to hearing words allows for a more participative prayer experience for all present.

Miming is a feature of this volume, comprising—in the Advent and Lent seasons—six of the 26 services. It allows us to express (for those who mime) and experience (for those who are watching) in action what is usually expressed only in words. In the mimed gospel scenes, I suggest some direction for the mimes, but only of a general nature so that the mimes can determine how they want to portray the narration. (See Dorothy Jonaitis's article in *Today's Parish* [January 1992] on the experience of putting miming to words. She describes how to write a script and how to use clothing, lighting, and music.)

As the Contents pages of this volume will reveal, these prayer services, covering liturgical seasons, civic holidays, and social occasions, are arranged more or less chronologically through the school year. Times when the services might suitably be used are suggested under the title of each service.

These prayer services may be adapted to other occasions as well, to celebrate or commemorate, say, events listed in *Chase's Annual Events: Special Days, Weeks & Months* (Contemporary Books, Chicago), which contains the dates of world and national days and months, such as Black History Month in February, United Nations World AIDS Day on December 1, Earth Day on April 21. The calendar in Copycat Press' bi-monthly publication is also helpful in recognizing special months or days of the year. Most elementary teachers are familiar with this publication.

Whether acting or miming, young people enjoy putting actions to words. This is more meaningful to them than only listening because they are more absorbed in what is happening in a prayer service, and if this helps them to reflect and pray better, then the opportunities for prayer in this volume are justified. It is my prayer that through these services young people may, like Samuel, grow more sensitive to God's call.

To encourage the widest participation by teenagers and staff alike, roles are generally not assigned for the speaking parts: Prayer, Scripture Reading, Response, Intercessions, Lord's Prayer, Blessing. In these sections of the prayer services, the leader should not only assign the speaking roles, but should also vary the assignments from one service to the other. For example, when a psalm is used as a Response, the verses may be recited alternately by right side and left side, or by Student 1, Student 2, Student 3, etc., or by the prayer leader, with the youths reciting the antiphon. In the Intercessions, one person may recite them all, or different people each may recite one. The first two prayer services exemplify this variety of assignments.

It is critical that the roles in this book be assigned sufficiently in advance so that the participants may prepare them well.

Where Scripture is to be mimed, presented in a dramatic reading, or otherwise enacted, the full text is presented. But if it is only read, it is recommended that this be done from a Bible or Lectionary; in which case the Scripture text is not given, but only the citation.

The Faith Reflection is a suggested line of thought that the speaker is to adapt and embellish. It is not meant to be read to the young people.

Directions to participants, such as in Ritual Action and other places, are given in italics and parentheses.

Finally, music is suggested on three occasions in each prayer service: the opening song, the responsorial, and the closing song. For the opening and closing songs, the leader is referred to a list of suggested sacred songs on pages 97-98. For the responsorial, a specific song is suggested in the text of the prayer service. A few categories of other music are also suggested to provide wider latitude in the selection.

New Beginning

Focus

To direct the youths' attention to academic achievement not as competition with others, but as striving to do the best and be the best students with the gifts God has given them

(Be sure that all assignments have been made and that all required materials are on hand.)

Opening Song

(See suggested songs in the Appendix.)

Prayer

Leader

God of creation and covenant,
we come together today as the community of (parish or school)
after spending long summer days
at work in the service of others
either at job or at home.
Open our minds
and allow our hearts to hear your holy word
and put it into action in our lives.
We ask this in the name of Jesus Christ, our Savior.

All

Amen.

Dramatic Reading

1 Samuel 3:1–21

(The narrator text in parentheses may be omitted.)

Narrator

Now the boy Samuel was ministering to the Lord under Eli. The word of the Lord was rare in those days; visions were not widespread. At that time Eli, whose eyesight had begun to grow dim so that he could not see, was lying down in his room; the lamp of God had not yet gone out, and Samuel was lying down in the temple of the Lord, where the ark of God was. Then the Lord called

Lord

Samuel! Samuel!

Narrator

(and he said)

Samuel

Here I am!

Narrator	and ran to Eli (and said)
Samuel	Here I am, for you called me.
Narrator	But he said
Eli	I did not call; lie down again.
Narrator	So he went and lay down. The Lord called again
Lord	Samuel!
Narrator	Samuel got up and went to Eli (and said)
Samuel	Here I am, for you called me.
Narrator	(But he said)
Eli	I did not call, my son; lie down again.
Narrator	Now Samuel did not yet know the Lord, and the word of the Lord had not yet been revealed to him. The Lord called Samuel again, a third time. And he got up and went to Eli (and said)
Samuel	Here I am, for you called me.
Narrator	Then Eli perceived that the Lord was calling the boy. (Therefore Eli said to Samuel)
Eli	Go lie down and if he calls you, you shall say, "Speak, Lord, for your servant is listening."
Narrator	So Samuel went and lay down in his place. Now the Lord came and stood there (calling as before)
Lord	Samuel! Samuel!
Narrator	(And Samuel said)
Samuel	Speak, for your servant is listening.
Narrator	(Then the Lord said to Samuel)
Lord	See I am about to do something in Israel that will make both ears of anyone who hears of it tingle. On that day I will fulfill against Eli all that I have spoken concerning his house, from beginning to end. For I have told

have spoken concerning his house, from beginning to end. For I have told him that I am about to punish his house forever, for the iniquity that he knew, because his sons were blaspheming God, and he did not restrain them. Therefore I swear to the house of Eli that the iniquity of Eli's house shall not be expiated by sacrifice or offering forever.

Narrator   Samuel lay there until morning; then he opened the doors of the house of the Lord. Samuel was afraid to tell the vision to Eli. But Eli called Samuel (and said)

Eli   Samuel, my son.

Narrator   (He said)

Samuel   Here I am.

Narrator   (Eli said)

Eli   What was it that he told you? Do not hide it from me. May God do so to you and more also, if you hide anything from me of all that he told you.

Narrator   So Samuel told him everything and hid nothing from him. (Then he said)

Eli   It is the Lord; let him do what seems good to him.

Narrator   As Samuel grew up, the Lord was with him and let none of his words fall to the ground. All Israel from Dan to Beersheba knew that Samuel was a trustworthy prophet of the Lord. The Lord continued to appear at Shiloh by the word of the Lord. And the word of Samuel came to all Israel.
            The word of the Lord.

All   Thanks be to God.

Responsorial
"Speak, Lord" (Dameans)
or Psalm 16:

All   You show me the path of life. In your presence there is fullness of joy; in your right hand are pleasures for evermore.

Leader   Protect me, O God, for in you I take refuge.
            I say to the Lord, "You are my Lord;
            I have no good apart from you."

All   You show me the path of life. In your presence there is fullness of joy; in your right hand are pleasures for evermore.

| Leader | As for the holy ones in the land, they are the noble, in whom is all my delight. Those who choose another god multiply their sorrows; their drink offerings of blood I will not pour out or take their names upon my lips. |

| All | You show me the path of life. In your presence there is fullness of joy; in your right hand are pleasures for evermore. |

| Leader | The Lord is my chosen portion and my cup; you hold my lot. The boundary lines have fallen for me in pleasant places; I have a goodly heritage. |

| All | You show me the path of life. In your presence there is fullness of joy; in your right hand are pleasures for evermore. |

| Leader | I bless the Lord who gives me counsel; in the night also my heart instructs me. I keep the Lord always before me; because he is at my right hand, I shall not be moved. |

| All | You show me the path of life. In your presence there is fullness of joy; in your right hand are pleasures for evermore. |

| Leader | Therefore my heart is glad, and my soul rejoices; my body also rests secure. For you do not give me up to Sheol, or let your faithful one see the Pit. |

| All | You show me the path of life. In your presence there is fullness of joy; in your right hand are pleasures for evermore. |

Gospel
Matthew 5:13–16

| All | Praise to you, Lord Jesus Christ. |

Faith Reflection

Like Samuel, we are called to share the talents God has given each of us. These gifts are meant to be used to make the world a better place, more like the Kingdom of peace and justice we believe God meant the world to be. The teachers use their talents in service of the students. The students should make use of these gifts and the gifts of their own ability to learn to improve themselves and make the world a better place. Education is a cooperative endeavor of teacher and students using the talents God has given to each; it is not a competition to determine who is better than another. Challenge those present, students and teachers, to share their talents for the good of all. Like the light on the hill in the gospel, our gifts do little good if kept hidden and secret.

Principal's Address
(Connecting the readings to the purpose of education, the principal should stress the administration's support of the students' reason for being in school.)

Ritual Action
Acts of Commitment

Principal Those involved in the administration and education of students at _____, please stand.

Faculty Based on our education, responsibility, and employment as administrators and teachers and with Jesus as the first teacher among us, we commit ourselves to be faithful and fair always in a peaceful classroom and school.

Principal You may be seated. Those enrolled as students at _____, please stand.

Students Based on our need to learn as students, we promise to be faithful students, to remember that education and learning come before all other school activities and events. We promise to strive for academic excellence under your guidance always in a peaceful classroom and school.

Enrollment Ceremony *(optional)*
(While instrumental music is playing, students sign up according to grade levels or homerooms at lecterns. Teachers might stand near the lectern of the class they instruct. Enrollment lists are displayed as a sign of their commitment to education.)

Intercessions
Response: Help us, O Lord.

Student 1 For peace in our world, we pray . . .

All Help us, O Lord.

Student 2 For unity in our Church, we pray . . .

All Help us, O Lord.

Student 3 For love in our neighborhoods, we pray . . .

All Help us, O Lord.

Student 4	For strength in our families, we pray . . .
All	Help us, O Lord.
Student 5	For courage in our lives, we pray . . .
All	Help us, O Lord.

Lord's Prayer

Blessing

Leader	As God called Samuel in the quiet of a gentle wind
	and as Jesus called his disciples to share his light to the world,
	may we go forth to be faithful teachers and students.
	Lord, help us always to remember
	that we are your servants
	and all that we do, we do in your name.
	This we ask through Christ our Lord.
All	Amen.

Closing Song

(See suggested songs in the Appendix. The school song might be sung.)

Work

Focus

To appreciate the gift of work as participants in creation and to petition for just and fair employment

(Be sure that all assignments have been made and that all required materials are on hand.)

Opening Song

(See suggested songs in the Appendix.)

Prayer

Leader   Compassionate and gentle God,
as Jesus and his disciples worked
to minister among people in need,
may our prayer today encourage us
to work diligently at the jobs
to which we are called;
give perseverance to those who look for employment.
We make this prayer according to your holy will.

All   Amen.

Reading

Genesis 1:26–31

All   Thanks be to God.

Response

Psalm 85: "Let Us See Your Kindness" (Haugen)
or Psalm 121:

All   I lift up my eyes to the hills—from where will my help come?

Left Side   My help comes from the Lord,
    who made heaven and earth.
He will not let your foot be moved;
    he who keeps you will not slumber.
He who keeps Israel
    will neither slumber nor sleep.

All   I lift up my eyes to the hills—from where will my help come?

Right Side	The Lord is your keeper;
	the Lord is your shade at your right hand.
	The sun shall not strike you by day,
	nor the moon by night.
All	I lift up my eyes to the hills—from where will my help come?
Left Side	The Lord will keep you from all evil;
	he will keep your life.
	The Lord will keep your going out and your coming in
	from this time on and forevermore.
All	I lift up my eyes to the hills—from where will my help come?

Gospel
Matthew 4:12–17

All	Praise to you, Lord Jesus Christ.

Faith Reflection
Just as Jesus began his "work" of ministry after his baptism and the time he spent in the desert, we are called to prayer and to work. Our work should be seen as ministry in service to our brothers and sisters in the Lord. Whatever our work or employment calls us to do, we should see it as making the world a better place, more like the Kingdom of God.

Ritual Action
(Representatives of various occupational groups process with items from their profession, which are placed in the sanctuary or central location. Reflective music might be played during this ritual.)

Intercessions
Response: We give you thanks, O Lord.

Leader	For all of creation . . .
All	We give you thanks, O Lord.
Leader	For work at home . . .
All	We give you thanks, O Lord.
Leader	For work at school . . .
All	We give you thanks, O Lord.

Leader	For our parents' jobs . . .
All	We give you thanks, O Lord.
Leader	For fair employment for all . . .
All	We give you thanks, O Lord.
Leader	For our ability to provide for those unable to work . . .
All	We give you thanks, O Lord.
Leader	For the opportunity to build up your kingdom . . .
All	We give you thanks, O Lord.

Lord's Prayer

Blessing

Student	Lord of work and play, through the gift of creation you have given us the opportunity to work, to improve our world. Bless the work of our hands and the times we take to rest from work. Watch over and protect those who are unemployed and their families. May we assist them in their endeavors to find just and fair employment. Guide employers to be good and faithful witnesses to your love. This we ask through Christ our Lord.
All	Amen.

Closing Song
(See suggested songs in the Appendix.)

Gratitude for Learning

Focus
To give thanks for knowledge learned and prepare for a restful and safe vacation from school

(Be sure that all assignments have been made and that all required materials are on hand.)

Opening Song
(See suggested songs in the Appendix.)

Prayer

Leader   Faithful God,
you have brought us together as the community of (school)
to thank you for the opportunity we have had to learn.
Through our prayer today,
grant us a peaceful, restful, and safe vacation
from our studies and school activities.
We ask this in your holy and glorious name.

All   Amen.

Reading
1 Corinthians 12:1–11

All   Thanks be to God.

Responsorial
"Blest Be the Lord" (Schutte)
or Psalm 18:

Response: The Lord is my rock, my fortress, and my deliverer, my rock in whom I will take refuge.

The cords of death encompassed me; the torrents of perdition assailed me;
     the cords of Sheol enabled me; the snares of death confronted me.
In my distress I called upon the Lord; to my God I cried for help.
     From his temple he heard my voice, and my cry to him reached his ears.

He reached down from on high, he took me;
     he drew me out of mighty waters.
He delivered me from my strong enemy, and from those who hated me;
     for they were too mighty for me.

They confronted me in the day of my calamity;
but the Lord was my support.
He brought me out into a broad place;
he delivered me, because he delighted in me.

The Lord rewarded me according to my righteousness;
according to the cleanness of my hands he recompensed me.
For I have kept the ways of the Lord,
and have not wickedly departed from my God.

Gospel
Luke 10:21–24

All   Praise to you, Lord Jesus Christ.

Faith Reflection
Paul reminds the Corinthians—and us—that there are many gifts, but they are all from the same Holy Spirit. Each of us is called to use the gifts we have been given to the best of our ability. Referring to the accomplishments of this grading period, remind the students that they did their best according to their abilities. As Jesus rejoiced with his disciples over what they learned, so too teachers and students should rejoice over what they have accomplished together using their gifts. *(A teacher or student might be invited to reflect on the importance of thanking God for learning and knowledge, possibly emphasizing something learned in the recent grading period.)*

Ritual Action
(Students process to the sanctuary or central location with items used in their studies as an offering of thanks for what they have learned. Another option for a ritual might be for the teachers to process to the sanctuary or central location with items used in their teaching. Reflective music might be played during this ritual.)

Intercessions
Response: Lord, watch over us.

When we are at prayer . . .
When we are at work or study . . .
When we are with our families and friends . . .
When we are at rest or sleeping . . .
When we are playing . . .

Lord's Prayer

Blessing

Lord of life and love,
as you rejoiced at the knowledge gained by your disciples,
so too rejoice with us at the end of this (period of time, or event).
May we rest peacefully
and safely during this vacation
so that we might return refreshed
to be faithful students once again.
This we ask through Christ our Lord.

All   Amen.

Closing Song

(See suggested songs in the Appendix.)

Using Our Gifts

Focus
To remind the performers or athletes that gifts come from God. Gifts should be used always to build up God's kingdom on earth.

(Be sure that all assignments have been made and that all required materials are on hand.)

Opening Song
(See suggested songs in the Appendix.)

Prayer
God of joy and grace,
as Jesus reminds us to use our gifts and talents
to build up the church,
may our prayer today remind us
that it does not matter whether we win or lose, succeed or fail.
What does matter is that we do our best
using the talents you have given us,
and appreciate the gifts of others,
for they all come from you, our loving God.
We ask this in Jesus' name.

All   Amen.

Reading
Philippians 3:12–16

Responsorial
Psalm 31 "I Put My Life in Your Hands" (Haugen)
or Psalm 16:

Response: Protect me, O God, for in you I take refuge.

Protect me, O God,
    for in you I take refuge.
I say to the Lord, "You are my Lord;
    I have no good apart from you."

As for the holy ones in the land,
    they are the noble, in whom is all my delight.
Those who choose another god
    multiply their sorrows;

Their drink offerings of blood I will not pour out
    or take their names upon my lips.

The Lord is my chosen portion and my cup;
    you hold my lot.
The boundary lines have fallen for me in pleasant places;
    I have a goodly heritage.

I bless the Lord who gives me counsel;
    in the night also my heart instructs me.
I keep the Lord always before me;
    because he is at my right hand,
        I shall not be moved.

Therefore my heart is glad, and my soul rejoices;
    my body also rests secure.
For you do not give me up to Sheol,
    or let your faithful one see the Pit.

You show me the path of life.
    In your presence there is fullness of joy;
in your right hand are
    pleasures for evermore.

Gospel
Mark 10:35–45 (or Matthew 20:20–28)

All   Praise to you, Lord Jesus Christ.

Faith Reflection
We are "to press toward the goal," as Paul challenges us. Each of us is fulfilled when we accomplish a goal. Jesus upset the thinking of the world by commanding us to serve the least among us, to put others before ourselves. The goal of our Christian life is not a prize or trophy but eternal life earned in serving the needs of our brothers and sisters. Athletic competition and artistic performances allow us to serve others with the gifts we have been given. Praying to win or poor sports conduct does not benefit anyone. Pray instead to do your best in the arts and in sports.

Ritual Action
(Those who are performing or competing together form a circle and recite a pledge or prayer together. The words of the Olympic Pledge would be appropriate.)

Intercessions
Response: Lord, hear us.

For a good performance . . .
For a safe game, match, or meet . . .
For the best use of our talents . . .
For good sports manners . . .
For respect of each other . . .
For more cooperation and less competition . . .

Lord's Prayer

Blessing

Good and faithful God,
may our prayer today guide us to a good performance.
May we use the gifts you have given us
to praise you and build up your kingdom on earth.
Whether we win or lose, succeed or fail,
guide us always to do your will
and be of service to our brothers and sisters always.
This we ask through Christ our Lord.

All   Amen.

Closing Song
(See suggested songs in the Appendix.)

Choose Life

Focus
To encourage respect for all life, especially for the lives of those closest to us

(Be sure that all assignments have been made and that all required materials are on hand.)

Opening Song
(See suggested songs in the Appendix.)

Prayer
God of all creation,
you created us and the world to express love.
Help us to love you and others as ourselves.
Through our prayer today,
may we come to appreciate the life
you have given us and the lives of all those we are called to love.
We make this prayer according to your life-giving will.

All   Amen.

Reading
Deuteronomy 30:11–20

All   Thanks be to God.

Responsorial
Psalm 19 "Lord, You Have the Words" (Haas)
or Psalm 139:

Response: I praise you, Lord, for I am wonderfully made.

O Lord, you have served me and known me.
You know when I sit down and when I rise up;
   you discern my thoughts from far away.
You search out my path and my lying down,
   and are acquainted with all my ways.

Even before a word is on my tongue,
   O Lord, you know it completely.
You hem me in, behind and before,
   and lay your hand upon me.

Such knowledge is too wonderful for me;
    it is so high that I cannot attain it.

Where can I go from your spirit?
    Or where can I flee from your presence?
If I ascend to heaven, you are there;
    if I make my bed in Sheol, you are there.
If I take the wings of the morning
    and settle at the farthest limits of the sea,
    even there your hand shall lead me,
    and your right hand shall hold me fast.

If I say, "Surely the darkness shall cover me,
    and the light around me become night,"
even the darkness is not dark to you;
    the night is as bright as the day,
    for darkness is as light to you.

For it was you who formed my inward parts;
    you knit me together in my mother's womb.
I praise you, for I am fearfully and wonderfully made.
    Wonderful are your works; that I know very well.
My frame was not hidden from you, when I was being made in secret,
    intricately woven in the depths of the earth.

Your eyes beheld my unformed substance.
    In your book were written all the days that were formed for me,
    when none of them as yet existed.
How weighty to me are your thoughts, O God!
    How vast is the sum of them!
I try to count them—they are more than the sand;
    I come to the end—I am still with you.

Gospel
John 15:1–11
or Matthew 22:34–40

All   Praise to you, Lord Jesus Christ.

Faith Reflection
Through Moses the Old Testament law was given to us: Choose life! Jesus also commanded that we love God and our neighbor as we love ourselves. Choosing life is shown by how we treat others, especially those closest to us, our families and friends. Each time we show love to others, we are choosing to live and to respect the life God has given to them and us.

Ritual Action
(Gather those present into a circle. Invite each person to face the person to their right and anoint their forehead with oil while saying, "May this anointing remind you of the life God has given you.")

Intercessions
Response: Lord, help us to love.

When we lack appreciation for our life . . .
When we show disrespect for the life of others . . .
When we cannot see God in creation . . .
When we become complacent to love . . .

Lord's Prayer

Blessing
God of life and love,
you have blessed us with life
and an appreciation for the life around us.
With the strength of the Holy Spirit,
may our self-respect lead always to love and respect for all life.
This we ask through Christ our Lord.

All   Amen.

Closing Song
(See suggested songs in the Appendix.)

From Death to Life

Focus
To assist the school or parish community in their grief and offer hope by Christ's promise of resurrection

(Be sure that all assignments have been made and that all required materials are on hand.)

Opening Song
(See suggested songs in the Appendix.)

Prayer
Lord of life,
as the community of (parish or school)
we gather to pray for (name of deceased) who has died.
Give us this time to mourn and comfort one another
with our belief in Christ's resurrection.
We ask this through your risen Son, Jesus Christ.

All   Amen.

Reading
Romans 6:1–11

All   Thanks be to God.

Responsorial
Psalm 23:

Response: The Lord is my shepherd, I shall not want.

He makes me lie down in green pastures;
    he leads me beside still waters;
    he restores my soul.
He leads me in right paths
    for his name's sake.

Even though I walk through the darkest valley,
    I fear no evil;
for you are with me;
    your rod and your staff—they comfort me.

You prepare a table before me in the presence of my enemies;

you anoint my head with oil; my cup overflows.
Surely goodness and mercy shall follow me
   all the days of my life,
and I shall dwell in the house of the Lord
   my whole life long.

All The Lord is my shepherd, I shall not want.

Gospel
John 14:1–6

All Praise to you, Lord Jesus Christ.

Faith Reflection
Paul preaches that we have already died in Christ through baptism. Our belief in Christ assures us of rising with him. Jesus gave us concrete examples of how we should live our lives: in the service of others, especially the disadvantaged. Jesus has prepared a place for us in God's Kingdom where he will welcome us into our inheritance. *(The principal or a teacher should offer concrete examples of how the life of the deceased youth imitated Jesus' life and example. Examples of how the school community might keep the memory of the deceased alive might be included. The young people should have the opportunity to express their own grief by telling stories of the deceased or writing them down. In this way the deceased person will live on in their hearts.)*

Ritual Action
(Teenagers are given a piece of paper to write a farewell message to the deceased. Roll them together with a ribbon and either place in the casket or give to the family. An optional ritual might be for them to write down a word or couple of words that could then be read while reflective music is played.)

Intercessions
Response: Lord, have mercy.

For _____ , who touched our lives, we pray . . .
For all of us in our grief and mourning, we pray . . .
For strength during these and other difficult times, we pray . . .
For perseverance in our daily struggles, we pray . . .
For all of our beloved deceased, we pray . . .

Lord's Prayer

Blessing

Almighty and life-giving God,
you alone give life
and you alone call us to perfection in your presence.
Be merciful to (name of deceased)
who has gone to his (her) peace in Christ.
Strengthen our faith and belief in you and in the resurrection.
Allow us to help one another
with the assurances of our faith
until we all meet (name of deceased)
and are with you and all who have died in your peace.
This we ask through Christ our Lord.

All   Amen.

Closing Song

(See suggested songs in the Appendix.)

Giving Thanks

Focus
To give thanks for all that God has given us, especially our **parents and families**

(Be sure that all assignments have been made and that all required materials are on hand.)

Opening Song
(See suggested songs in the Appendix.)

Prayer
Gracious and generous God,
As the community of (school or parish),
we gather to give you thanks
for all the gifts we have been given
individually and as a community.
We give special thanks for our parents and families.
May we never forget to offer you thanks and praise
for all that you provide for us.
We ask this through the greatest gift, Jesus Christ our Savior.

All   Amen.

Reading
2 Corinthians 1:3–7

All   Thanks be to God.

Responsorial
Psalm 145 "I Will Praise Your Name" (Haas)
or Psalm 33:

Response: Rejoice in the Lord!

Rejoice in the Lord, O you righteous.
   Praise befits the upright.
Praise the Lord with the lyre;
   make melody to him with the harp of ten strings.
Sing to him a new song;
   play skillfully on the strings with loud shouts.

For the word of the Lord is upright,
   and all his work is done in faithfulness.

He loves righteousness and justice;
    the earth is full of the steadfast love of the Lord.

By the word of the Lord the heavens were made,
    and all their host by the breath of his mouth.
He gathered the waters of the seas as in a bottle;
    he put the deeps in storehouses.

Let all the earth fear the Lord;
    let all the inhabitants of the world stand in awe of him.
For he spoke, and it came to be;
    he commanded, and it stood firm.

Gospel
Matthew 11:25–30

All   Praise to you, Lord Jesus Christ.

Faith Reflection
Giving thanks is very common in the Scriptures. Paul gave thanks to God even for the trouble he had in his life. Jesus thanked God often and reminded his disciples and us to do the same. By acknowledging what God has given to us and done for us, we express our gratitude. Some days it is easy to be thankful; at other times we tend to forget what we have received. A day like "Thanksgiving Day" almost forces us to be thankful. The word "Eucharist" means "to give thanks." Challenge those present to be aware of one gift or treasure for which they are especially thankful. Ask them to show their gratitude for this soon.

Ritual Action
(The teenagers write down what they are thankful for on a small piece of paper. Collect the folded pieces of paper into a basket or baskets and have the basket(s) lifted high during the intercessions.)

Intercessions
Response: We give you thanks, O Lord.

For the beauty of creation . . .
For our very life which comes from you alone . . .
For our ancestors and our freedom . . .
For our families and especially our parents . . .
For our friends . . .

Lord's Prayer

Blessing

Faithful and giving God,
as Paul thanked God constantly
for the people given to him as a sign of blessing,
we too thank you for all your gifts to us.
With your help and strength,
may we always be grateful
for all you have given us and done for us.
This we ask through Christ our Lord.

All   Amen.

Closing Song

(See suggested songs in the Appendix.)

Prophet, Voice of God

Mime Service for Advent

Focus

To emphasize the role of the prophets in the history of the Jewish and Christian peoples. Special emphasis is placed upon the messages of Isaiah, Jeremiah, and John the Baptist, but includes the message of other prophets as well.

(Be sure that all assignments have been made and that all required materials are on hand.)

(The church is darkened. A light shines on Narrator 1, mimes are hidden around stage area.)

Narrator 1   God had already made the heavens and the earth, the sky and the sea, the birds, fish and animals, and humans too. The flood had come and gone. Moses had already given the Ten Commandments to the Jewish people and they entered the Promised Land. The Judges and Kings had ruled the chosen people for many centuries. Invaders had ravaged the people and the land. Once again, the people found themselves feeling alone, abandoned, and aching for God. *(Lights on stage. Mimes enter walking back and forth across the stage)*

Narrator 2   The people rushed about as if they didn't have a care or concern in the world. They were oblivious to God and to one another's needs. They went about fast and furious without bothering to help or assist anyone. They seemed to have stopped paying attention to God or to one another. The poor got poorer and the widowed and orphaned were hungry and tired of being neglected. And then one of them, at God's bidding, spoke up above the noise of the rest.
(Isaiah stands amongst the crowd while the crowd continues to walk in slow motion back and forth across the stage.)

Isaiah   Hear, O heavens and listen, O earth,
    for the Lord speaks:
Children I have raised and reared,
    but they have disowned me!
An ox knows its owner,
    and a mule, its master's manger;
But Israel does not know,
    my people has not understood.
Ah, sinful nation, people laden with wickedness,
    evil race and corrupt children!

Come, now, let us set things right,
    says the Lord:

Though your sins be like scarlet,
  they may become white as snow:
Though they be crimson red,
  they may become white as wool.
If you are willing and obey,
  you shall eat the good things of the land:
But if you refuse and resist,
  the sword shall consume you:
  for the mouth of the Lord has spoken!
(Isaiah 1:2–4,18–19)
(Crowd continues to move at a regular pace, Isaiah huddles to the floor.)

Narrator 2   The one who spoke was named Isaiah. But the people did not stop their business; they didn't even hear Isaiah's voice. They paid no attention. The poor were neglected; the widow and the orphan were forgotten.

(Mimes freeze in their places momentarily; a mime portrays the poor, one the widow, and another the orphan. They walk together from one side of the stage to the other while other mimes are still frozen in place. The poor, widow, and orphan mimes are searching for people to assist them in their need.)

Narrator 3   When the poor, the widow, and the orphan are forgotten, God cries, it is said. God did not intend anyone to be forgotten. That was why God gave more to some than to others. God wanted to see if we would share. God had shared so much with us when the world was created: the land, animals, other people, and God's own image. God never imagined that we would forget the needs of people. For so many of us, however, it is so easy to forget the people God wants us to remember. The poor cry out for attention to their needs, the widow cries out for protection, and the child cries out for love and safety. When we do not help these people, we are not helping God who we believe dwells in each person. Though we might forget these people, God never forgets them.

(Mimes walk slowly off stage while "Isaiah 49" by Carey Landry is played. Singing along may be encouraged.)

(A few mimes walk slowly back and forth across the stage.)

Narrator 1   God tried again, thinking that maybe the people would listen if he insisted or emphasized part of the message. God again commanded the people to listen to the voice and act on the words of the one who spoke.
(Isaiah stands among the people as they continue to walk back and forth.)

Isaiah   The Lord will give you this sign: the virgin shall be with child and bear a son. His name shall be Emmanuel which means "God is with us." *(One of the mimes stands still and watches Isaiah speaking.)*

The people who walked in darkness have seen a great light;
    Upon those who dwell in the land of gloom, a light has shone.
You have brought them abundant joy and great rejoicing,
    As they rejoice before you as at the harvest, as they make merry
    when dividing spoils.
For the yoke that burdened them, the pole on their shoulder,
    And the rod of their taskmaster you've smashed, as on the day
    of Midian.
For every boot that tramped on battle, every cloak rolled in blood,
    will be burned as fuel for flames. *(Another mime stands still
    and watches Isaiah.)*
For a child is born to us, a son is given us;
    upon whose shoulder dominion rests.
They name him Wonder-Counselor, God-Hero, Father-Forever,
    Prince of Peace.
His dominion is vast and forever peaceful,
    From David's throne and over his kingdom, which he confirms
    and sustains
By judgment and justice both now and forever. *(Another mime
    stands still and watches Isaiah.)*

Narrator 1   It was amazing, as Isaiah spoke, that some actually stood and listened to his words. Some of the people were really paying attention. Isaiah became excited and continued to challenge them to care for others, especially the poor, widowed, and orphaned children.

Narrator 2   But what was it about these other people who seemed not to care about anyone but themselves? As Isaiah continued to speak, he thought of how he might get others interested in helping him get the message out. He would ask those who seemed to care to listen for God's voice in their own lives as he had listened in his life. *(Isaiah points to one listening and they trade places. Other mimes continue to walk back and forth slowly.)*

Jeremiah   Return, rebel Israel, says the Lord,
    I will not remain angry with you;
For I am merciful, says the Lord,
    I will not continue my wrath forever.
Only know your guilt:
    how you rebelled against the Lord, your God,
How you ran hither and yon to strangers under every green tree
    and would not listen to my voices, says the Lord.
Return rebellious children, says the Lord,
    for I am your Master;
I will take you, one from a city, two from a clan;
    and bring you to Zion.
(Jeremiah 3:12–14)

Narrator 2   Jeremiah continued to announce his powerful message. He called the people back to faithfulness to God and to the covenant they had agreed upon. He also reminded them of God's love for them, a love they didn't return. But even the hearts of those who heard the message hardened. *(One by one those listening join the other mimes who continue to walk back and forth, ignoring Jeremiah as he continues to speak.)* They lost interest and grew tired of being faithful. It is was easier to just do what each one wanted to do, easier to be stubborn and disobedient. *(All mimes huddle to the floor.)*

Narrator 3   When our hearts harden, God's spirit in the world decreases, love disappears, and forgiveness is no longer. Has your heart hardened over your relationship with God, with another person, or within yourself? We know the difference between hard hearts and loving, kind, forgiving hearts. *(A few mimes step away from the crowd and begin to act out the following:)* Have you not forgiven God for something that was not God's fault? Have you been angry with God because you did not win a game or get a promotion? Did you ever apologize to God for the last time you got angry with God? Is your heart hard because you cannot forgive your friend? Have you ever forgiven your parents for anything? Have you denied forgiveness when asked? Are you still so angry at someone, you don't ever think you'll forgive him or her? When was the last time you asked for someone's forgiveness? How can you deny another the forgiveness that the Lord asks you to offer? Are you angry with yourself? Are you sorry for something you said when you should have kept your mouth closed? Or is it that you cannot forgive yourself for what you did to hurt someone? Hard hearts lead to closed ears, eyes, and arms. Then we close ourselves off to God's presence in the person next to you. If you let go of what bothers and upsets you, your heart will have a chance to be softened.

(Mimes walk swiftly back and forth across the stage. Jeremiah stands amongst them while three mimes watch and listen to him.)

Narrator 2   Jeremiah continued to speak God's message to the people. Be faithful to God for God has been faithful to you. Remember the covenant God made with us. God gave Jeremiah the words to speak against the neighboring lands that wanted to invade Jerusalem and take the people into exile. But again the people did not listen and their hearts were hardened. *(The three mimes join the other mimes walking back and forth. Jeremiah soon joins them.)* Nebuchadnezzar and the army of Babylon encamped around Jerusalem. *(Some mimes gather the rest together in a crowd.)* They built a seige wall around the city. *(Mimes inside the crowd bend down while the mimes around them raise their hands slowly.)* Famine, war, and insurrection plagued Jerusalem. The soldiers and the people fled into the hill country. They were trapped and cried out to God whom they believed had abandoned them again. Nebuchadnezzar led his army and the rest of the people in Jerusalem into exile.

(Mimes on the outside move those inside off the stage area to a place close by that can be seen by some of the people with mimes inside remaining bent down and inside the circle.)

Narrator 1   But while the people were exiled, Baruch, Jeremiah's secretary, rose from amongst the people. *(Mimes all kneel around and look up at Baruch.)*

Baruch   The Lord fulfilled the warning he had uttered against us, against our judges, our kings, our princes, and against all of Israel and Judah. God has made us subject to all the nations around us. We are brought low because we sinned against the Lord, our God, not heeding his voice. And now, God of Israel, take your anger from us, for we are few in number among the nations to which you scattered us. Hear, O Lord, our prayer of supplication and have mercy on us who have sinned against you.

Narrator 1   And Ezekiel rose up amongst the people to speak God's message to them while they dwelled in a foreign land. *(Ezekiel stands among the crowd while all listen.)* Ezekiel spoke first of the destruction of Jerusalem and then about the new Israel that would rise from among the exiled.

Ezekiel   The hand of the Lord came upon me and brought me in divine visions to the land of Israel, where he set me down on a very high mountain. On it a city seemed to be built before me. When God brought me there, all at once I saw a man who appeared like bronze, standing in the gate, holding a linen cord and measuring rod. The man said, "Son of man, look carefully and listen intently, and pay strict attention to all I will show you, for you have been brought here so that I might show it to you. Tell the house of Israel all that you see." *(Mimes, still on their knees, move back to the stage area while Ezekiel continues speaking.)*

Narrator 1   Ezekiel continued to relay God's message to the people in exile. He spoke of the restored temple in Jerusalem and how each person was expected to be faithful to God because God would once again save them from their sins of unfaithfulness.

Narrator 2   *(Ezekiel kneels with the people while Daniel stands to speak.)* Daniel was another prophet who spoke to the people while in Babylonian captivity. He even attempted to interpret King Nebuchadnezzar's dream to save the wise men of Babylon from being put to death. *(Daniel kneels with the people while Hosea stands to speak.)* Hosea, a prophet from the northern kingdom, compared the relationship between God and the people with the relationship between spouses. God was faithful to the people, but they were not faithful in return. The people were beginning to get anxious about God saving them again from exile. *(Mimes stand up one by one and begin to walk away from Hosea.)*

Other prophets proclaimed God's message. Amos, Jonah, Micah, Habakkuk, Haggai, Zechariah, Malachi, and many others attempted to make the people see how sinful their infidelity was. Many died in exile, but those who returned to Jerusalem thrived and rebuilt their homes and communities. There they were still unfaithful, even as God continued to protect them.

(Mimes all walk back and forth again across the stage beginning to walk hunched over or on their knees. John the Baptist stands tall among the people.)

John Repent, for the kingdom of heaven is at hand! Reform your lives; the Lord, our Messiah, is coming!

Narrator 1 *(Mimes continue to move back and forth ignoring John.)* The people once again ignored God's message spoken through John. He was known as the Baptizer because his baptism was for the forgiveness of sin. *(John invites a few mimes to step down from the stage area with him to be baptized.)*

John Repent, for the kingdom of heaven is at hand! Reform your lives; the Lord, our Messiah, is coming! I baptize you for the forgiveness of your sins.

Narrator 1 Some of the people remembered the words of Isaiah.

Isaiah A voice will cry out in the desert, "Prepare the way of the Lord; make straight his paths. Prepare the way. Prepare the way."

Song "Prepare Ye the Way of the Lord" from *Godspell*

(Mimes mouth the words and clap, move among the people to get them to stand, sing and participate in the clapping. After singing the refrain a couple of times, instruments keep playing during the following:)

Narrator 1 And the people began to talk among themselves about the strength of his message. They asked him:

Narrator 2 Are you the Messiah? Are you Elijah or the prophet?

John One mightier than I is coming after me. I am not worthy to stoop and loosen his sandals. I have baptized you with water, but he will baptize you with the Spirit. "Prepare the way of the Lord; make straight his paths. Prepare the way. Prepare the way." *(Music continues and singing resumes.)*

(Lights dim and John leads all off the stage area singing "Prepare Ye the Way of the Lord" from Godspell.)

Celebrating Confirmation
Acceptance, Enrollment, and Commitment

Focus

To recognize and celebrate the journey of faith that members of our parish community are making toward the celebration of the sacrament of Confirmation

(Be sure that all assignments have been made and that all required materials are on hand.)

Opening Song
(See suggested songs in the Appendix.)

Greeting and Welcome

Prayer

Lord, giver of all gifts,
you bless us with your divine life
and with abilities and talents according to your Spirit.
As we listen to your holy word,
strengthen our resolve to serve you in our brothers and sisters.
Guide us on our journey of faith to the sacrament of Confirmation.
We ask this through Christ our Lord.

All   Amen.

Reading
Acts of the Apostles 2:1–13

Responsorial
"You Are Near" (Schutte)

Gospel
Matthew 28:16–20

All   Praise to you, Lord Jesus Christ.

Faith Reflection

Since the apostles were given the gifts of the Spirit and since Jesus promised he would be with us through the Holy Spirit, a youth leader or catechist should reflect on how Jesus is alive and among us and how the Holy Spirit is present in our actions and words: by bringing life and love to others. A recent example from the news would assist the young people to see how one can share their gifts in everyday life. These rites allow the community to recognize the journey of faith and celebrate that journey within the parish community.

Ritual Action
Rite of Acceptance

Leader   (Pastor or Confirmation Coordinator's name [P/CC]), I present to you the Candidates of our parish community who are requesting to begin their preparation for the sacrament of Confirmation. Already baptized into Christ, they freely choose to follow Jesus more closely by entering into this preparation process. To help them in this process they turn to you and the parish community of (parish name) for support, encouragement, and guidance.

P/CC   Members of the parish community, you have heard the request for our guidance and support. If you are willing to help these young people by your witness of Christian living and by your prayers, please say "We are."

All   We are.

P/CC   Parents and families, if you are willing to continue to give that special encouragement these candidates will need from you in their continuing Christian journey, please say "We are."

Parents and
Families   We are.
          (Candidates for acceptance stand.)

P/CC   Confirmation candidates, do you make a special choice today to enter into (continue) the process of preparation for the sacrament of Confirmation?

Cand   We do.

P/CC   Do you freely choose to try to follow the gospel teachings that are being presented to you?

Cand   We do.

P/CC   Do you promise to study, to pray, to serve, and to build community in order to become a young adult witness to Jesus Christ?

Cand   We do.

P/CC   We, the parish of (parish name), pledge to support you in your decision and look forward to the day of your Confirmation.

Rite of Enrollment

Leader (Pastor or Confirmation Coordinator's name), I present to you our Confirmation candidates who seek to deepen their commitment and become full members of their church by receiving the sacrament of Confirmation. They have been faithfully attending preparation sessions over the past two years, have engaged in service projects to the community, and participated in retreat days. As they enter into the final phase of their preparation, I ask that our parish community affirm them by accepting their names for enrollment.

P/CC Are you willing to verify for the parish community of (parish name) that there is a real sense of commitment to following Jesus' way of life within the Roman Catholic church?

Leader I am.

P/CC Parents and families, if you are willing to continue to give that special encouragement these candidates will need from you in their continuing Christian journey, please say "We Are."

Parents and Families We are.
(Candidates for enrollment stand.)

P/CC Young people of our parish, are you willing to continue the process of Christian initiation begun in you at Baptism and continued in the Eucharist?

Cand We are.

P/CC Do you understand that the sacrament of Confirmation symbolizes not a completion of your religious education, but rather a mature commitment to continue to grow spiritually as Christian adults?

Cand We do.

P/CC Then may God bring to completion in you the good work that has begun in Jesus Christ. I invite you to come forward and enroll your name in our parish book of candidates.

(Candidates walk to one of the stands at the front of the main aisle and sign his or her name.)

Rite of Commitment

Leader (Pastor or Confirmation Coordinator's name), the day of Confirmation is drawing near and so these candidates whom I now present to you are completing their period of preparation. They have found strength in God's grace and support in our community's prayers and examples. Now they ask that they be allowed to participate in the sacrament of Confirmation.

P/CC   Those who are to be confirmed on (date), please come forward when your name is called.

(Candidates come forward as their names are called, take a candle from the table in front of the altar and stand side by side facing the people in front of the sanctuary steps.)

My dear friends, these candidates have asked to complete their initiation into the life of the church. Those who know them have judged them to be sincere in their desire. During the period of their preparation, they have listened to the word of God and endeavored to follow his commands; they have shared the company of their Christian brothers and sisters and joined them in prayer; and so I announce to all of you here that our community has decided to call them to the sacrament of Confirmation. Now I ask you, the members of (parish name): If you are willing to affirm the testimony expressed about these candidates and support them in faith, prayer, and example, please say "We are."

All   We are.

P/CC   Now, my dear candidates, since you have already heard the call of Christ, you must now express your response clearly and in the presence of the this community. Therefore, do you wish to enter fully into the life of the church through the sacrament of Confirmation?

Cand   We do.

P/CC   Then take and receive this light as a remembrance of the candle your parents held for you at your own Baptism. In the sacrament of Confirmation, you have chosen to accept the light of faith. May this light continue to burn in your life and guide you on your journey of faith. May sin and sickness be burned away by the light of this candle. And when the Lord comes, may you with this light, go out to meet him with all the saints in the heavenly kingdom. We ask this through Christ our Lord.

All   Amen.

Intercessions
Response: "Lord, send us your Spirit."

When we are at work and at home . . .
When we are at school and studying . . .

When we are alone or with others . . .
When we are challenged for what we believe . . .
When we try to live as Jesus taught us . . .
When we use the gifts of the Holy Spirit given to us . . .

Lord's Prayer

Blessing and Dismissal
God of faithfulness and mercy,
grant us strength and perseverance
as we make our journey in faith.
May the gifts of the Holy Spirit
given to each of us
allow us to keep your Son Jesus alive in the world
through our words and actions.
We ask this through Christ our Lord.

All   Amen.

Closing Song
(See suggested songs in the Appendix.)

Living Water
Mime Service for Lent

Focus
To recognize the gift of our faith and to encourage those present to use their gifts in the way God intended them to be used

(Be sure that all assignments have been made and that all required materials are on hand.)

Narrator 1   *(Mimes are off stage area; stage is lighted.)* According to John's gospel, Jesus had to pass through Samaria, and his journey brought him to a Samaritan town named Shechem near the plot of land that Jacob had given to his son Joseph. *(Jesus walks to the center of the stage area and sits.)* This was the site of Jacob's well. Jesus, tired from his journey, sat down at the well. At about noon, a Samaritan woman came to draw water. *(Coming from the opposite side of the stage area, the Samaritan woman stands next to Jesus.)*

Jesus   Give me a drink.

Samaritan   You are a Jew. *(Points to Jesus and crosses arms.)* How can you ask me, a Samaritan and a woman, for a drink?

Jesus   If only you recognized God's gift, and who it is that is asking you for a drink, you would have asked him instead, and he would have given you living water.

Samaritan   Sir, you don't have a bucket and this well is deep. *(Points with hands to the well.)* Where do you expect to get this flowing water? Surely you don't pretend to be greater than our ancestor Jacob, who gave us this well and drank from it with his sons and his flocks? *(Mimes freeze in place.)*

(Mimes enter to act out the following by showing their hands cupped as if they were carrying something valuable and offer it to one another. As they offer it to others, they then carry it and offer it too. Action continues through this narration.)

Narrator 3   Do you recognize God's gift to you? Where do you find the gifts God has given to you and your family? Each of us has been given a well deep and rich with God's gifts. Our life's goal is to search and uncover the gifts God has placed in each of our wells. Your gift may be compassion or understanding, patience or perseverance in difficult times. Maybe you have been given the gift of saying or writing something thoughtful to one who needs encouragement. Is your family, spouse, or children your greatest gift? Have you ever thought of a good friend as a gift from God that has been placed in your well? All of these gifts are part of the living water God has given you for eternal life. *(Mimes, except for Jesus and woman, exit stage.)*

Jesus Everyone who drinks this water will be thirsty again. But whoever drinks the water I give will never be thirsty; no, the water I give shall become a fountain within, leaping up to provide eternal life.

Samaritan Give me this water, sir, so that I won't grow thirsty again and have to keep coming here to draw water.

Jesus Go, call your husband and then come back here.

Samaritan I have no husband.

Jesus You are right in saying you have no husband! The fact is, you have had five, and the man you are living with now is not your husband. What you said is true enough.

Samaritan *(Moving close to Jesus)* Sir, I can see you are a prophet. Our ancestors worshiped on this mountain, but you people claim that Jerusalem is the place where people ought to worship God.

Jesus *(Jesus stands up and woman steps away from Jesus.)* Believe me, woman, an hour is coming when you will worship the Father neither on this mountain nor in Jerusalem. You people worship what you do not understand, while we understand what we worship. Yet an hour is coming, and is already here, when authentic worshipers will worship the Father in Spirit and truth. Indeed, it is just such worshipers the Father seeks. God is Spirit, and those who worship God must worship in Spirit and truth.

Samaritan I know there is a Messiah coming. When he comes, he will tell us everything.

Jesus I who speak to you am he.

Narrator 1 *(Disciples move into the sanctuary.)* The disciples of Jesus, returning at this point, were surprised that Jesus was speaking with a woman. The woman left her water jar and went off into the town to tell everyone.

Samaritan Come and see someone who told me everything I ever did! Could this not be the Messiah?

Narrator 1 *(People move into the sanctuary.)* With that, everyone set out to meet him. Meanwhile the disciples were encouraging Jesus to eat something.

Jesus I have food to eat of which you do not know.

Narrator 1   The disciples wondered if someone had brought Jesus something to eat.

Jesus   Doing the will of him who sent me and bringing his work to completion is my food. Do you not have a saying: "Four months more and it will be harvest time"? Listen to what I say: Open your eyes and see! The fields are shining for harvest! The reaper already collects his wages and gathers a yield for eternal life, that sower and reaper may rejoice together. Here we have the saying verified: "One person sows; another reaps." I sent you to reap what you had not worked for. Others have done the labor, and you have come into their gain. *(Mimes freeze in place.)*

Narrator 3   Do you know God's will for you? Have you tried to learn what it means for you in your particular circumstances? *(Some of the mimes begin to mime the following narration by praying and showing kindness to others.)* God's will is communicated to us in prayer, in quiet moments, through others. Do you allow God to speak to you, or have you had difficulty hearing God in your life? Are there noises and voices in your life that are drowning out God's voice? Is doing God's will your food, your nourishment? Opening our eyes and listening are how we can keep in touch with God's will for us. The harvest of God's will is rich for you. Have you reaped more than you planted or are you still hungry for God's will in your life? *(All mimes join together kneeling around Jesus as he teaches them.)*

Narrator 1   Many Samaritans from that town believed in Jesus on the strength of the woman's testimony. The result was that, when these Samaritans came to him, they begged him to stay with them awhile. So he stayed there two days and through his own spoken word many more came to faith. *(Mimes slowly move Jesus off the stage area.)*

Narrators   No longer does our faith depend on your story. We have heard for ourselves, and we know that this really is the savior of the world. *(All mimes exit stage.)*

Narrator 1   The gospel of the Lord.

All   Praise to you, Lord Jesus Christ.

Faith and Sight
Mime Service for Lent

Focus
To appreciate the unity and diversity in God's creation, especially in human beings

(Be sure that all assignments have been made and that all required materials are on hand.)

Narrator 1   *(A blind person is sitting center stage, while Jesus and his disciples walk by him and stop.)* According to John's gospel, as Jesus walked along, he saw a man who had been blind from birth. His disciples questioned Jesus: *(One of the disciples looks toward Jesus.)*

Disciples   Rabbi, was it his sin or his parents' that caused him to be born blind?

Jesus   Neither. It was no sin, either of this man or his parents. Rather, it was to let God's works show forth in him. We must do the deeds of the one who sent me while it is day. The night comes on when no one can work. While I am in the world, I am the light of the world.

Narrator 1   With that, Jesus spat on the ground, made mud with his saliva, and smeared the man's eyes with the mud. *(Jesus touches the ground and touches the blind person's eyes.)*

Jesus   Go wash in the pool of Siloam.

Narrator 1   So the man went off and washed and came back able to see. *(The blind person turns back and then around with open eyes while neighbors enter and Jesus and his disciples exit. Crowd enters and faces the person born blind. Mimes act out the following.)* His neighbors and the people who had been accustomed to seeing this person beg questioned his presence.

Narrator 2   Isn't this the one who used to sit and beg?

Narrator 1   Some were claiming it was; others maintained it was not, but someone who looked similar.

Blind Person   I am the one, all right.

Narrator 2   How were your eyes opened?

Blind Person	That man they call Jesus made mud and smeared it on my eyes, telling me to go to Siloam and wash. When I did go and wash, I was able to see.
Narrator 2	Where is he?
Blind Person	I have no idea.
Narrator 1	*(Crowd moves the person born blind off the stage.)* Next they took the one who had been born blind to the Pharisees. Because Jesus cured on the Sabbath, the Pharisees began to inquire how this person could now see.
Blind Person	He put mud on my eyes. I washed it off and now I can see.
Narrator 2	He cannot be from God because he does not keep the sabbath.
Narrator 3	But if one is a sinner, how can he perform signs like these?
Narrator 2	Since it was your eyes he opened, what do you have to say about him?
Blind Person	He is a prophet.
Narrator 1	The Jews refused to believe that he had really been born blind and had begun to see, until they summoned his parents.
Narrator 2	Is this your child and if so, do you attest that your child was blind at birth? How do you account for the fact that your child now can see?
Narrator 3	We know this is our child, and we know our child was blind at birth. But how our child's sight was restored, or who opened our child's eyes, we have no idea. Ask our child who is old enough to speak.
Narrator 1	The parents of the one blind from birth were afraid of the Jews, who had already agreed among themselves that anyone who acknowledged Jesus as the Messiah would be put out of the synagogue. The Pharisees again summoned the one born blind.
Narrator 2	Give glory to God! First of all, we know this man who you say healed you is a sinner.
Blind Person	I would not know whether he is a sinner or not. I know this much: I was blind before; now I can see.

Narrator 2   Just what did he do to you? How did he open your eyes?

Blind
Person   I have told you once, but you would not listen to me. Why do you want to hear it all over again? Do not tell me you want to become his disciples too?

Narrator 2   You are the one who is that man's disciple. We are disciples of Moses. We know that God spoke to Moses, but we have no idea where this man comes from.

Blind
Person   Well, this is news! You do not know where he comes from, yet he opened my eyes. We know that if someone is devout and obeys, God listens to them. It is unheard of that anyone ever gave sight to a person blind from birth. If this man were not from God, he could never have done such a thing.

Narrator 2   What! You are steeped in sin from your birth, and you are giving us lectures?

Narrator 1   With that, they brought the man born blind out bodily. *(Crowd takes the person born blind away. Other mimes act out the following by making fun of handicapped people or people different from themselves.)*

Narrator 3   Have you hurt someone close to you with a derogatory comment? Have you made fun of someone who is blind or deaf, someone with a different skin color, or who spoke a language unfamiliar to you? God made the world with many different kinds of people with different skin colors, languages, and customs to show us the variety of creation. Just imagine a world where we were all the same. How boring and tired we would get of one another. God blessed the world with variety. God challenged us not to ignore people who are different than we are. We should instead make attempts to get along with one another. *(Person born blind walks across stage area.)*

Narrator   When Jesus heard that the person born blind had been thrown out of the synagogue, he looked for him. *(Jesus walks up to the person born blind.)*

Jesus   Do you believe in the Son of Man?

Blind
Person   Who is he, sir, that I may believe in him?

Jesus   You have seen him. He is speaking to you now.

Blind
Person   I do believe, Lord. *(Person born blind bows at Jesus' feet.)*

Jesus   I came into this world to divide it, to make the sightless see and the seeing blind. *(Pharisees enter the stage and face Jesus.)*

Narrator 1 Some of the Pharisees overheard this.

Narrator 2 You are not counting us in with the blind, are you?

Jesus   If you were blind, there would be no sin in that. "But we see" you say and your sin remains. *(Jesus and person born blind exit to one side of the stage while Pharisees exit the other side of stage.)*

Narrator 1 The gospel of the Lord.

All   Praise to you, Lord Jesus Christ.

New Life
Mime Service for Lent

Focus
To put our trust in God when sickness or death touches our life

(Be sure that all assignments have been made and that all required materials are on hand.)

Narrator 1 *(Lights on stage.)* According to John's gospel, there was a certain man named Lazarus who was sick. He was from Bethany, the village of Mary and her sister Martha. Mary was the one who had anointed the Lord with perfume and dried his feet with her hair. The sisters sent word to Jesus to inform him that Lazarus was sick. *(Jesus and disciples enter the stage. Jesus is teaching them.)*

Jesus This sickness is not to end in death; rather it is for God's glory, that through it the Son of God may be glorified.

Narrator 2 Jesus loved Martha, Mary, and Lazarus very much. Yet after hearing that Lazarus was sick, he stayed on where he was for two days more. Finally he informed his disciples that they should go back to Judea.

Disciples But Jesus, with the Jews only recently trying to stone you, are you going back there again?

Jesus Are there not twelve hours of daylight? If a man goes walking by day he does not stumble, because he sees the world bathed in light. But if he goes walking at night he will stumble, since there is no light in him. Our beloved Lazarus has fallen asleep, but I am going there to wake him.

Disciples Lord, if he is asleep, his life will be saved.

Jesus Lazarus is dead. For your sakes I am glad I was not there, that you may come to believe. In any event, let us go to him. *(Jesus and disciples freeze. Other mimes enter to act out the following narration by attending to the sick and suffering.)*

Narrator 3 Does your lack of faith at times cause you to not believe in God's power to forgive sin, cure sickness, or even raise people from the dead? So often we question God's power to work in our world because people do get sick and die. If it were our will, no one would get sick or die. When we are affected by sickness or death, our faith should be strengthened. We should put trust in God and less trust in human ability. God's healing and power can be seen even when sickness and death seem to take hold. Instead of turning away from God, these should be times when we turn to God and believe! *(Mimes leave stage.)*

Thomas Let us go along, to die with him. *(Jesus and disciples move to one edge of the stage area and walk around to the opposite side of the stage during the following:)*

Narrator 1 When Jesus arrived in Bethany, he found that Lazarus had already been in the tomb four days. The village was not far from Jerusalem, just under two miles, and many people had come out to console Martha and Mary over their brother. When Martha heard that Jesus was coming, she went to meet him while Mary sat at home. *(Martha goes out to meet Jesus and disciples. Martha takes Jesus' hands.)*

Martha Lord, if you had been here, my brother would never have died. Even now, I am sure that God will give you whatever you ask.

Jesus Your brother will rise again.

Martha I know he will rise again, in the resurrection on the last day.

Jesus I am the resurrection and the life: whoever believes in me, though he should die, will come to life; and whoever is alive and believes in me will never die. Do you believe this?

Martha Yes, Lord, I have come to believe that you are the Messiah, the Son of God: he who is to come into the world. *(Martha moves to the opposite side of the stage area.)*

Narrator 1 Martha went back to the house and called her sister Mary.

Martha The teacher is here asking for you.

Narrator 1 *(Mary and the Jews go out to meet Jesus. Mary falls at Jesus' feet.)* Mary and those who were consoling her got up quickly and went out. They thought she was going to the tomb to weep. When Mary came to Jesus, she fell at his feet.

Mary Lord, if you had been here, my brother would never have died.

Narrator 1 When Jesus saw her weeping, and those who had accompanied her also weeping, he was troubled in spirit and moved by the deepest emotions.

Jesus Where have you laid him?

Narrator 2 Lord, come and see. *(Mimes move to another part of the stage area.)*

Narrator 1	Jesus began to weep.
Narrator 2	See how much he loved him! He opened the eyes of that blind man. Why could he not have done something to stop this man from dying?
Narrator 1	Once again, troubled in spirit, Jesus approached the tomb.
Jesus	Take away the stone.
Martha	Lord, it has been four days now; surely there will be a stench!
Jesus	Did I not assure you that if you believed you would see the glory of God? Father I thank you for having heard me. I know that you always heard me but I have said this for the sake of the crowd, that they may believe that you sent me. Lazarus, come out! *(Lazarus enters the stage area as if he is asleep.)*
Narrator 1	The dead man came out, bound hand and foot with linen strips, his face wrapped in a cloth.
Jesus	Untie him and let him go free. *(Mimes freeze in place while other mimes enter to act out the following narration by showing how we reject and let others down.)*
Narrator 3	What causes us to not believe God has the power to save us from death? Giving up on someone or something is a kind of death. Have you given up on someone lately? Were they relying on you and you let them down, sort of dying on them? Part of us dies when we feel that we cannot do something the way someone else does it. Instead of dying and giving up, we should come to life and learn how we might assist them in their task. We should never die at our attempts to become more caring people and never give up responding to God's invitation to new life. *(Mimes leave the stage while Jesus the others continue.)*
Narrator 1	This caused many of the Jews who had come to console Mary, and had seen what Jesus did, to put their faith in him. *(Pause)* The gospel of the Lord. *(Mimes exit.)*
All	Praise to you, Lord Jesus Christ.

Reconciliation
Mime Service for Lent

Focus
To celebrate and imitate the unconditional and loving forgiveness of God

(Be sure that all assignments have been made and that all required materials are on hand.)

Narrator 1 *(Stage is lit. A lone voice sings "Jesus, remember me when you come into your kingdom" by Roc O'Connor. Some mimes are listening to Jesus off to one side of the stage area.)* The tax collectors and sinners were all drawing near to listen to him, but the Pharisees and scribes began to complain.

Narrator 2 This man welcomes sinners and eats with them.

Narrator 1 So he addressed this parable to them. *(Mimes sit around Jesus.)*

Jesus *(Shepherd enters the stage area looking for a sheep.)* What man among you having a hundred sheep and losing one of them would not leave the ninety-nine in the desert and go after the lost one until he finds it? *(Shepherd finds the sheep and rejoices, carrying it across the stage.)* And when he does find it, he sets it on his shoulders with great joy and, upon his arrival home *(Shepherd calls together family and friends.)*, he calls together his family and neighbors and says to them, "Rejoice with me because I have found my lost sheep." *(Jesus and disciples freeze at one side of the stage. Shepherd acts out the following narration by wandering around the stage looking lost and forsaken by family and friends.)*

Narrator 3 Have you ever felt lost and alone in the world? Have you ever felt that no one understood you or cared about you? Have you ever felt that there was no direction in your life? Often, because of a tragic or frightening experience, we can feel alone and lost. Jesus tells us often that he will find us when we are lost. We should want Jesus to find us so that he can care for us and forgive us of whatever caused us to become lost. *(Shepherd exits while Jesus continues with the disciples.)*

Jesus I tell you, in just the same way there will be more joy in heaven over one sinner who repents than over ninety-nine righteous people who have no need of repentance.

Narrator 1 Jesus continued to tell them another parable. *(Woman enters the stage area looking for lost coins.)*

Jesus What woman having ten coins and losing one would not light a lamp and sweep the house, searching carefully until she finds it? And when she does find it, she calls together her *(Woman calls people toward her and rejoices with them.)* friends and neighbors and says to them, "Rejoice with me because I have found the coin I lost." *(Jesus and disciples freeze while a woman acts out the following narration by acting superior to those who are lost in the world, snubbing her nose and looking down at others.)*

Narrator 3   Have you forgotten or neglected those who are lost in our world? There are many poor people who feel lost or alone. Though Jesus has told us the poor will always be with us, we must respond to their needs so that they don't have to feel lost and lonely and lack what they need for a decent life. How have you helped someone poor . . . hungry . . . homeless . . . widowed . . . oppressed? By helping them with physical needs we can make them feel more a part of the human family. In this way, we are spreading the good news that has enriched our lives and saved us from the sin of neglecting God's least ones. *(Woman exits while Jesus and disciples continue.)*

Jesus   In just the same way, I tell you, there will be rejoicing among the angels of God over one sinner who repents.

Narrator 1   Then Jesus told them yet another parable.

Jesus   A man had two sons and the younger son went to his father. *(Father and sons enter the stage area while the disciples sit around Jesus.)*

Narrator 2   Father, give me the share your estate that should come to me.

Narrator 1   So the father divided the property between them. *(Prodigal son gathers items and goes to one side of the stage area.)* After a few days the younger son collected all his belongings and set off to a distant country where he squandered his inheritance on a life of dissipation. When he had freely spent everything, a severe famine struck that country, and he found himself in dire need. So he hired himself out to one of the local citizens who sent him to his farm to tend the swine. And he longed to eat his fill of the pods on which the swine fed, but nobody gave him any. *(Prodigal son looks forlorn and unhappy.)* Coming to his senses he thought, "How many of my father's hired workers have more than enough food to eat, but here am I, dying from hunger. I shall get up and go to my father and I shall say to him, 'Father I have sinned against heaven and against you. I no longer deserve to be called your son; treat me as you would treat one of your hired workers.'" So he got up and went back to his father. *(Mimes freeze in place while the prodigal son acts out the following narration by swearing and cursing to heaven and then acting remorseful.)*

Narrator 3   Do you recognize the wrongness of your actions or words? Do you have a difficult time realizing that some of what you say or do is not according to

God's law? When you speak of God disrespectfully, do you admit it and attempt to correct your speech? When you disobey your parents, are you sorry? Do you show remorse and ask forgiveness? Do you worship regularly at the Eucharist? Have you appreciated what God has given you, or do you long to have what is another's? Have you obeyed the Ten Commandments? Loved God and your neighbor as yourself? *(Mimes continue.)*

Narrator 1 *(Father sees prodigal son, runs toward him and embraces him.)* While he was still a long way off, his father caught sight of him, and was filled with compassion. He ran to his son, embraced him, and kissed him.

Narrator 2 Father, I have sinned against heaven and against you; I no longer deserve to be called your son.

Narrator 1 *(Father gives orders to servants.)* But his father ordered his servants to quickly bring the finest robe and put it on him; put a ring on his finger and sandals on his feet. "Take the fattened calf and slaughter it. Then let us celebrate with a feast, because this son of mine was dead and has come to life again; he was lost and has been found." Then the celebration began. *(Older son off to the side of the stage area sees what is going on and speaks to a servant.)* Now the older son had been out in the field and, on his way back, as he neared the house, he heard the sound of music and dancing. He called one of the servants and asked what this might mean.

Narrator 2 Your brother has returned and your father has slaughtered the fattened calf because he has him back safe and sound.

Narrator 1 The older son became angry, and when he refused to enter the house, his father came out and pleaded with him. *(Father and older son stand together.)*

Narrator 2 Look, all these years I served you and not once did I disobey your orders; yet you never gave me even a young goat to feast on with my friends. But when your son returns who swallowed up your property with prostitutes, for him you slaughter the fattened calf.

Narrator 3 My son, you are here with me always; everything I have is yours. But now we must celebrate and rejoice, because your brother was dead and has come to life again; he was lost and has been found. *(All mimes exit.)*

Narrator 1 The gospel of the Lord.

All Praise to you, Lord Jesus Christ.

Walking With Jesus
Stations of the Cross

Focus
To walk the way of the cross with Jesus through contemporary situations and applications

(Be sure that all assignments have been made and that all required materials are on hand.)

(The church is in darkness except for necessary lights over music area. Narrators are positioned, one at each of four microphones at the side of the sanctuary if possible. Sanctuary is clear of everything movable, leaving space for the crucifixion and placement of the cross as well as mimes. All actors wear black or dark colored clothing. Jesus wears white shorts with an alb over top. The only props are a large cross that can be carried and placed in a stand and hammers or mallets. The song "Show Me the Way" by Styx can be appropriately used with this mime prayer service.)

Scene 1
JESUS INSTRUCTS HIS DISCIPLES
(Jesus and disciples enter sanctuary area from the back of the church during instrumental music. All take a seat around Jesus in the sanctuary; lights are on in sanctuary area.)

Narrator 1   Jesus in the company of his disciples instructed them in these words,

Jesus   Do not let your hearts be troubled. Believe in God; believe also in me. In my Father's house there are many dwelling places. If it were not so, would I have told you that I go to prepare a place for you? And if I go to prepare a place for you, I will come back again and will take you to myself, so that where I am, there you may be also. And you know the way to the place where I am going.

Narrator 1   Thomas said to Jesus,

Speaker   Lord, we do not know where you are going. How can we know the way?

Jesus   I am the way, and the truth, and the life. No one comes to the Father except through me. If you know me, then you will know my Father. From now on, you do know him and have seen him. (John 14:1–7)

(All move off the sanctuary toward congregation area and are seated during instrumental music.)

Scene 2

THE GARDEN

(Judas and Jesus face each other while disciples are seated around them.)

Narrator 1 Jesus went out with his disciples across the Kidron Valley to a place where there was a garden, which he and his disciples entered. Now Judas, who betrayed him, also knew the place, because Jesus often met there with his disciples. So Judas brought a detachment of soldiers together with police from the chief priests and Pharisees, and they came there with lanterns and torches and weapons. Then Jesus, knowing all that was to happen to him, came forward and asked,

Jesus Who are you looking for?

Speaker Jesus of Nazareth.

Jesus I am he.

Narrator 2 The soldiers stepped back and fell to the ground. Again he asked,

Jesus Who are you looking for?

Speaker Jesus of Nazareth.

Jesus I told you that I am he. So if you are looking for me, let these men go. (John 18:1–11)

Narrator 2 So the soldiers, their officer, and the Jewish police arrested Jesus *(Soldiers arrest Jesus and lead him off.)* and bound him. First they took him to Annas, who was the father-in-law of Caiaphas, the high priest that year. Caiaphas was the one who had advised the Jews that it was better to have one person die for the people. *(Mimes move to the back of the church or are seated on the floor during the contemporary application.)*

Narrator 1 *(In the sanctuary area, lights shine on mimes making fun of others for their physical differences.)* People are condemned every day to a certain kind of death. They are condemned because of the color of their skin, the language they speak, the religion they practice, or because of some other differences. The unfortunate error of all these condemnations is that there are more characteristics that unite human beings than there are that separate us. Who of us when we were created were asked if we would like to speak a certain language, be born in a particular country, be given a specific skin color, or be raised by a family in a definite religion? We all have more in common with one another than we have unique to ourselves. Our society and world point out our differences while God celebrates our being members of a community called the human family. *(Contemporary mimes are seated in the sanctuary.)*

Scene 3
HIGH PRIEST'S COURTYARD
(Jesus faces Annas and is being held by the soldiers, while Peter stands with the servants some distance away.)

Narrator 1   Simon Peter and another disciple followed Jesus. Since that disciple was known to the high priest, he went with Jesus into the courtyard of the high priest, but Peter was standing outside at the gate. So the other disciple, who was known to the high priest, went out, spoke to the woman who guarded the gate, and brought Peter in. The woman said to Peter,

Speaker   You are not also one of this man's disciples, are you?

Narrator 2   I am not.

Narrator 1   Now the slaves and the police had made a charcoal fire because it was cold, and they were standing around it and warming themselves. Peter also was standing with them and warming himself. Then the high priest questioned Jesus about his disciples and about his teaching. Jesus answered,

Jesus   I have spoken openly to the world; I have always taught in synagogues and in the temple, where all the people come together. I have said nothing in secret. Why do you ask me? Ask those who heard what I said to them; they know what I said.

Narrator 1   When he had said this, one of the police standing nearby struck Jesus on the face, (saying)

Speaker   Is that how you answer the high priest?

Narrator 1   (Jesus answered)

Jesus   If I have spoken wrongly, testify to the wrong. But if I have spoken rightly why do you strike me?

Narrator 1   Then Annas sent him bound to Caiaphas the high priest. Now Simon Peter was standing and warming himself. They asked him,

Narrator 2   You are not also one of his disciples, are you?

Narrator 1   (He denied it and said)

Speaker   I am not.

Narrator 1   One of the slaves of the high priest, a relative of the man whose ear Peter had cut off, asked,

Narrator 2   Did I not see you in the garden with him?

Narrator 1   Again Peter denied it, and at that moment the cock crowed.
              (John 18:12–27)

              (Mimes move slowly toward next station while congregation sings a familiar Lenten refrain like "Jesus, Remember Me.")

Scene 4
PILATE'S HEADQUARTERS
(Jesus, held by soldiers, faces Pilate, both standing, while his disciples and other soldiers are seated or kneeling on the floor around them.)

Narrator 2   Then they took Jesus from Caiaphas to Pilate's headquarters. It was early in the morning. They themselves did not enter the headquarters, so as to avoid ritual defilement and to be able to eat the Passover. So Pilate went out to them (and said)

Speaker   What accusation do you bring against this man?

All   If this man were not a criminal, we would not have handed him over to you.

Speaker   Take him yourselves and judge him according to your law.

All   We are not permitted to put anyone to death.

Narrator 2   Then Pilate entered the headquarters again, summoned Jesus, and asked,

Speaker   Are you the King of the Jews?

Jesus   Do you ask this on your own, or did others tell you about me?

Speaker   Your own nation and the chief priests have handed you over to me. What have you done?

Jesus   My kingdom is not from this world. If my kingdom were from this world, my followers would be fighting to keep me from being handed over. But as it is, my kingdom is not from here.

Speaker   So you are a king?

Jesus   You say that I am a king. For this I was born, and for this I came into the world, to testify to the truth. Everyone who belongs to the truth listens to my voice.

Speaker	What is truth?
Narrator 1	After he had said this, he went out to the Jews again (and told them)
Speaker	I find no case against him. But you have a custom that I release someone for you at the Passover. Do you want me to release for you the King of the Jews?
All	Not this man, but Barabbas!
Narrator 1	*(Soldiers hit Jesus and place a crown on his head.)* Then Pilate took Jesus and had him flogged. And the soldiers wove a crown of thorns and put it on his head, and they dressed him in a purple robe. They kept coming up to him, (saying)
All	Hail, King of the Jews!
Narrator 1	(and) striking him on the face. Pilate went out again (and said to them)
Speaker	Look, I am bringing him out to you to let you know that I find no case against him.
Narrator 1	So Jesus came out, wearing the crown of thorns and the purple robe. (Pilate said to them)
Speaker	Here is the man!
Narrator 1	When the chief priests and the police saw him, they shouted,
All	Crucify him! Crucify him!
	(Soldiers take Jesus away, hand him the cross, and lead him away slowly.)
Pilate	Take him yourselves and crucify him; I find no case against him. (John 18:28–19:6)

Scene 5
JESUS FALLS THE FIRST TIME
(Jesus falls, the cross is held by the soldiers, and then rested upon Jesus on the floor.)

Narrator 2	Under the heavy weight of the timbers on his shoulders, Jesus fell to the ground. The soldiers and guards who accompanied him whipped him and beat him.

(Lights go on in sanctuary. Jesus and soldiers freeze in place.)

Narrator 1   (*In the sanctuary, mimes act out people leaving babies and children and sending children away.*) Young children are often the first victims of an unjust society or of unfit parents. A baby is abandoned on a city street by a frightened, unmarried mother. Parents of a young child are abducted, put in a camp, or murdered. Other parents and their young family try to escape by boat from an oppressive country and their boat capsizes and they drown. Millions of children are crushed by starvation, physical and sexual abuse, abortion, poverty, war, migration, and corruption in an uncaring society. Abandoned children show us our fallen humanity; they reveal our sins to us. Jesus continues to fall this day in the terrible fate of many children. Many children, not far from our homes, are beaten, starved, neglected, and mistreated. Do we have the courage to pick up the cross we have given them? Do we have the power to alleviate this cross in our world? Or do we simply feel that it is not our problem or concern? Each of us is a child of a loving God and God expects us to care for others as God has cared for us. (*Lights over the sanctuary are turned off.*)

Scene 6
JESUS MEETS HIS MOTHER

(*Jesus and soldiers resume walking and come to Mary. Jesus stops in front of her.*)

Narrator 2   Carrying the cross, Jesus came upon his mother, Mary, and a few of his disciples who were consoling her. She looked at him with deep sorrow in her eyes, for she knew that there was nothing she could do for him. The pain in her heart was so great; she wanted to take away his pain.

(*Jesus and soldiers walk slowly away from Mary while the congregation sings a familiar hymn or refrain.*)

Scene 7
SIMON HELPS JESUS

(*Simon meets Jesus while the soldiers kneel on one knee or sit down around them.*)

Narrator 2   As they led Jesus away, they seized a man, Simon of Cyrene, who was coming from the country, and they laid the cross on him, and made him carry it behind Jesus.

(*Simon helps Jesus carry the cross slowly while mimes in the sanctuary act out people helping others by giving them food, helping them walk, and being friendly.*)

Narrator 1   As Simon helped Jesus carry the cross, Jesus must have thought about all the people he had helped in his ministry: the couple and guests at the wedding feast in Cana, Nicodemus who came to him at night with questions about faith, the Samaritan woman at the well, multiplying the loaves and fishes for the crowd on the hill, forgiving the sins of the woman caught in adultery, curing the man born blind, raising Lazarus from the dead, washing the feet of his disciples, offering them bread and wine as his own body and blood, and commanding them to do this in his memory. All these things Jesus remembered as Simon helped carry the heavy cross. As Jesus was preparing to give of himself most completely by offering his very life, he accepted this last act of kindness from Simon of Cyrene. (Luke 23:26)

(Mimes in sanctuary move off slowly and Simon continues to assist Jesus carry the cross with soldiers walking slowly in front and behind them.)

Scene 8
JESUS MEETS VERONICA

(Jesus stops to speak with Veronica, as the soldiers again kneel or sit around them.)

Narrator 1   Veronica was a follower of Jesus and she witnessed him healing the sick and casting out the devil. She had come to believe that he was the Messiah, the Anointed, the Son of God. As she stood along the way watching Jesus carry the cross, she saw a tired and desperate human face. She wondered what she could do for him. *(Veronica wipes the sweat and blood off Jesus' face.)* She took her veil and wiped the sweat and blood off of his face. He smiled at her for her act of kindness. When she stepped away, Veronica saw the image of Jesus in blood and sweat on her veil and she cried.

(Jesus, Simon, and Veronica freeze. Mimes in the sanctuary look for their husbands and sons; some other mimes console the women.)

Narrator 2   "What have you done with my husband?" is the cry of women in some countries as they hold pictures of their missing husbands. All over the world, women, men, and children are looking for the "lost" wives, husbands, parents, and children. They have been told their relatives were a threat to the government. These women represent other women, men, and children who cannot locate loved ones due to violence and war. Even in our own country, loved ones are missing because of drugs, abortion, and sickness. There is immense pain in losing one who is loved. Their pain is our pain and we all cry out to God for comfort and relief. Our relief and comfort come from others who are God's arms, hands, and hearts for us. As we are comforted in our losses so must we comfort others. *(Mimes move out of sanctuary.)*

Scene 9
JESUS FALLS A SECOND TIME

(Jesus, Simon, and the soldiers continue on the way. Jesus falls again while the soldiers take the cross and place it on him.)

Narrator 1   Completely exhausted, Jesus falls a second time under the weight of the cross. His pain and suffering are not yet over and he realizes that as hard as this ordeal is, he must continue to carry out the will of his Father. He does not carry the cross for himself, but for all of us.

(Jesus gets up and continues carrying the cross while the congregation sings a familiar hymn or refrain.)

Scene 10
JESUS MEETS THE WOMEN OF JERUSALEM

(Jesus meets some women who are crying and trying to touch him, as the soldiers stand between Jesus and the women.)

Narrator 1   A great number of the people followed him, and among them were women who were beating their breasts and wailing for him. But Jesus turned to them (and said)

Jesus   Daughters of Jerusalem, do not weep for me, but weep for yourselves and for your children. For the days are coming when they will say, "Blessed are the barren, and the wombs that never bore, and the breasts that never nursed." Then they will begin to say to the mountains, "Fall on us," and to the hills, "Cover us." For if they do this when the wood is green, what will happen when it is dry? (Luke 23:27–31)

(Jesus, soldiers, and the women freeze in place while mimes in the sanctuary act out people being refused food, medicine, or shelter; those denied these things walk away slowly.)

Narrator 2   Who do we cry for in our world today? Thousands of human beings are dying of hunger each day. Malnutrition affects countless more. Millions are homeless in our world, our country, and in our city. So very many in the United States are without health care. Food, shelter, and medicine are not luxuries in our world, but necessities for being human. Do we cry for these people? Do we pray for these people? Do we act for these voiceless members of our society? Oh God, help us care for those less fortunate and in need. *(Mimes in sanctuary exit slowly.)*

Scene 11
JESUS FALLS A THIRD TIME

(Jesus falls again while the soldiers take the cross, place it on him, and kick him, and spit on him.)

Narrator 1   Nearly to the point of passing out, Jesus falls a third time with the heavy cross lying on top of him. He can almost go on no farther. The soldiers and guards whip him and spit upon him. They yell at him to get up and move on.

(Jesus gets up and continues carrying the cross while the congregation sings a familiar hymn or refrain.)

Scene 12
JESUS IS STRIPPED AT GOLGOTHA AND CRUCIFIED

(Jesus and the soldiers enter the sanctuary. Soldiers remove Jesus' alb. He is wearing white shorts. He lies down on the cross while the soldiers hammer the cross near his hands and feet. Soldiers divide his clothes and gamble for his tunic.)

Narrator 2   They crucified Jesus, and with him two others, one on either side. Pilate had an inscription written and put on the cross: "Jesus of Nazareth, the King of the Jews." Many read this inscription, because the place where Jesus was crucified was near the city; and it was written in Hebrew, in Latin, and in Greek. Then the chief priests said to Pilate, "Do not write, 'The King of the Jews,' but, 'This man said, I am King of the Jews.'" (Pilate answered)

Speaker   What I have written I have written.

Narrator 2   When the soldiers had crucified Jesus, they took his clothes and divided them into four parts, one for each soldier. They also took his tunic; now the tunic was seamless, woven in one piece from the top. So they said to one another, "Let us not tear it, but cast lots for it to see who will get it." This was to fulfill what the scriptures say, "They divided my clothes among themselves, and for my clothing they cast lots." And that is what the soldiers did.

Narrator 1   Meanwhile, standing near the cross of Jesus were his mother, and his mother's sister, Mary the wife of Clopas, and Mary Magdalene. When Jesus saw his mother and the disciple whom he loved standing beside her, he said to his mother,

Jesus   Woman, here is your son.

Narrator 1   Then he said to the disciple,

Jesus   Here is your mother.

Narrator 1   And from that hour the disciple took her into his own home. After this, when Jesus knew that all was now finished, he said (in order to fulfill scripture)

Jesus	I am thirsty.
Narrator 1	A jar full of sour wine was standing there. So they put a sponge full of the wine on a branch and held it to his mouth. When Jesus had received the wine, he said,
Jesus	It is finished.
Narrator 1	Then he bowed his head and gave up his spirit. (John 19:18–30)

(All freeze while loud music, organ music, or recorded thunder is played and the lights are turned off and on for 30 seconds simulating a storm.)

Scene 13
JESUS IS BURIED

(Jesus is taken down from the cross and carried down the aisle slowly by his disciples while the following is read. The cross may be placed at the foot of the sanctuary for veneration after the service.)

Narrator 2	After these things, Joseph of Arimathea, who was a disciple of Jesus, though a secret one because of his fear of the religious leaders, asked Pilate to let him take the body of Jesus. Pilate gave him permission; so he came and removed it. Nicodemus, who had at first come to Jesus by night, also came, bringing a mixture of myrrh and aloes, weighing about a hundred pounds. They took the body of Jesus and wrapped it with the spices in linen cloths, according to the burial custom. Now there was a garden in the place where he was crucified, and in the garden there was a new tomb in which no one had ever been laid. And so, because it was the day of Preparation, and the tomb was nearby, they laid Jesus there. (John 19:38–42)

(Mimes should go to a quiet place for prayer and reflection, apart from the congregation, so as to allow the congregation to leave in silence without congratulating the mimes.)

Bearing God's Gifts

Focus
To thank God for our abilities, particularly those for which awards are being given

(Be sure that all assignments have been made and that all required materials are on hand.)

Opening Song
(See suggested songs in the Appendix.)

Prayer
Lord our God,
as Jesus' passion and death
was followed by the resurrection,
may our prayer today remind us
that the work we do and the rewards we receive
are all God's gifts.
We make our prayer in your holy name.

All   Amen.

Reading
Philippians 3:12–16

All   Thanks be to God.

Responsorial
Psalm 145 "I Will Praise Your Name" (Haas)
or Psalm 8:

Response: O Lord, how majestic is your name in all the earth!

You have set your glory above the heavens.
   Out of the mouths of babes and infants
you have founded a bulwark because of your foes,
   to silence the enemy and the avenger.

When I look at your heavens, the work of your fingers,
   the moon and the stars that you have established;
what are human beings that you are mindful of them,
   mortals that you care for them?

Yet you have made them a little lower than God,
   and crowned them with glory and honor.

You have given them dominion over the works of your hands;
   you have put all things under their feet,
all sheep and oxen,
   and also the beasts of the field,
the birds of the air, and the fish of the sea,
   whatever passes along the paths of the sea.

Gospel
John 20:1–10

All   Praise to you, Lord Jesus Christ.

Faith Reflection
Paul likened our life to a race that all of us are running for the prize of eternal life. Simon Peter and the disciple John raced to witness the empty tomb: a sign of the eternal life Jesus offers to all of those who follow in his footsteps. Our challenge is to assist each other in the race to eternal life. Ceremonies like this one assist us to remember the greatness of the prize that will be ours because of our life in Christ Jesus.

Speeches and Award Presentations

Intercessions
Response: We give you glory, O Lord.

For the work and effort of each day . . .
For the sweat and tears of competition . . .
For the joy of winning . . .
For the pain of trying . . .
For the agony of defeat . . .
For the goals achieved . . .
For the perseverance to try again . . .

Lord's Prayer

Blessing
Faithful and loving God,
through the life, death, and resurrection
of your son, Jesus,
you have rewarded all with the gift of your glory.
May the work and awards of this day
always remind us of the reward of our faithful and loving lives.
This we ask through Christ our Lord.

All   Amen.

Closing Song
(See suggested songs in the Appendix.)

Just the Beginning

Focus
To thank God for the accomplishments of the graduates and to ask for God's blessing and protection upon them and their families

(Be sure that all assignments have been made and that all required materials are on hand.)

Procession Music
"Pomp and Circumstance" or another appropriate musical selection.

Prayer
Generous and forgiving God,
look upon our graduates and their families with love
and let them know your caring presence.
Bless our graduates for their accomplishments
and strengthen them so that they may put
the gifts you have given them to good use
as they give you thanks for them and for this day.
We ask this in your name.

All   Amen.

Reading
1 Peter 1:13–16

All   Thanks be to God.

Responsorial
Psalm 100 "We Are His People" (Haas)
or Psalm 138:

Response: I give you thanks, O Lord, with all my heart.

I bow down toward your holy temple
  and give you thanks to your name for your steadfast love
  and your faithfulness;
For you have exalted your name and your word
  above everything.

On the day I called, you answered me,
  you increased my strength of soul.
All the kings of the earth shall praise you, O Lord.
  for they have heard the words of your mouth.

They shall sing of the ways of the Lord,
> for great is the glory of the Lord.
For though the Lord is high, he regards the lowly;
> but the haughty he perceives from far away.

Though I walk in the midst of trouble,
> you preserve me against the wrath of my enemies;
you stretch out your hand,
> and your right hand delivers me.

The Lord will fulfill his purpose for me;
> your steadfast love, O Lord, endures forever.
Do not forsake the work of your hands.

Gospel
Luke 24:13–35

All   Praise to you, Lord Jesus Christ.

Faith Reflection
As Jesus calls us to recognize his presence in the breaking of the bread, so too we are called as his followers to recognize his presence in each other. A commencement is an end to a lot of hard work and a beginning of new adventures. In whatever the students choose to do, they will be called to recognize the work of Jesus in their work and the presence of Jesus in others.

(A speaker addresses the graduates and families on how the scripture reading and the graduates' accomplishments have prepared them for their lives ahead.)

Conferral of Diplomas

Song
(The school song would be appropriate.)

Intercessions
Response: Lord, hear our prayer.

For peace in our world and neighborhoods, we pray . . .
For love in our streets and our homes, we pray . . .
For unity in our church and our communities, we pray . . .
In thanksgiving for the education our graduates have received, we pray . .
For continued success and blessings on our graduates, we pray . . .

Lord's Prayer

Blessing

Loving God, as you made yourself known
to the disciples on the road to Emmaus,
make your holy presence and love known
in the work our graduates have accomplished.
Strengthen and guide them all their days.
May they always know the love you have for them
and may they share all they have learned
to build up your Kingdom.
This we ask through Christ our Lord.

All   Amen.

Closing Song

(See suggested songs in the Appendix.)

Making a Difference

Focus
To ask God's blessings and protection on those going to college

(Be sure that all assignments have been made and that all required materials are on hand.)

Opening Song
(See suggested songs in the Appendix.)

Prayer
Loving God,
as Jesus sent his disciples to minister to the world,
may our prayer today strengthen
those going to college
that they might see their studies
as a ministry of service to the world.
We ask this in your holy name.

All   Amen.

Reading
Jeremiah 1:4–10

All   Thanks be to God.

Responsorial
Psalm 27 "The Lord Is My Light" (Haas)
or Psalm 27:

Response: The Lord is my light and my salvation; whom shall I fear?

When evildoers assail me to devour my flesh—
    my adversaries and foes—they shall stumble and fall.
Though an army encamp against me,
    my heart shall not fear;
though war rise up against me,
    yet I will be confident.

One thing I asked of the Lord, that I will seek after:
    to live in the house of the Lord all the days of my life,
    to behold the beauty of the Lord, and to inquire in his temple.
For he will hide me in his shelter in the day of trouble.

he will conceal me under the cover of his tent;
  he will set me high on a rock.

Do not hide your face from me.
Do not turn your servant away in anger, you who have been my help.
  Do not cast me off, do not forsake me, O God of my salvation!
If my father and mother forsake me,
  the Lord will take me up.

Teach me your way, O Lord, and lead me on a level path
  because of my enemies.
Do not give me up to the will of my adversaries,
  for false witnesses have risen against me,
  and they are breathing out violence.

I believe that I shall see the goodness of the Lord
  in the land of the living.
Wait for the Lord; be strong, and let your heart take courage;
  wait for the Lord!

Gospel
Matthew 28:16–20

All Praise to you, Lord Jesus Christ.

Faith Reflection
Jeremiah claims he is too young to be a prophet. God's call for us to be his messengers can come to us at any time or any age. As Jesus sends his disciples to preach and heal, he assures them he will be with them. Beginning a new experience like college can be an exciting and overwhelming endeavor. Just as the disciples knew Jesus was with them, so too the college students must be assured that Christ is with them. (*A personal witness by a current college student may be appropriate.*)

Ritual Action
(*Parents and teachers or youth leaders raise hands over the youths during the intercessions as a form of blessing. Or another ritual action might be for the parents and teachers or youth leaders to lay hands on the youths and pray silently while reflective music is played.*)

Intercessions
Response: Protecting Lord, watch over us.

When we are alone . . .
When we feel abandoned . . .
When we think of our family and friends . . .

When we are studying . . .
When we are preparing for exams . . .
When we are sick and homesick . . .
When we travel . . .

Lord's Prayer

Blessing
Loving and protecting Lord,
watch over our friends as they go to college.
May they always be aware of your love for them.
Whether they feel joy or sadness,
shower them with your loving guidance
in their studies and other activities.
May the Holy Spirit fill their hearts
with a love for your commandments.
This we ask through Christ our Lord.

All   Amen.

Closing Song
(See suggested songs in the Appendix.)

In Need of Healing

Focus
To petition God to comfort and strengthen those who are sick, especially those in a terminal condition

(Be sure that all assignments have been made and that all required materials are on hand.)

Opening Song
(See suggested songs in the Appendix.)

Prayer
Healing and compassionate God,
as Jesus assured his disciples
that a person's faith was required for healing,
may our prayer assure us
that our faith in your healing power
will cure those who are sick or suffering from disease and illness.
We make this prayer according to your loving will.

All   Amen.

Reading
Romans 12:1–2

All   Thanks be to God.

Responsorial
Psalm 31 "I Put My Life in Your Hands" (Haugen)
or Psalm 33:

Response: Rejoice in the Lord!

Happy is the nation whose God is the Lord,
    the people whom he has chosen as his heritage.
The Lord looks down from heaven;
    he sees all humankind.

From where he sits enthroned he watches all the inhabitants of the earth—
    he who fashions the hearts of them all,
    and observes all their deeds.
A king is not saved by his great army;
    a warrior is not delivered by his great strength.

Truly the eye of the Lord is on those who fear him,
　　on those who hope in his steadfast love
　　to deliver their soul from death,
　　and to keep them alive in famine.

Our soul waits for the Lord;
　　he is our help and shield.
Our heart is glad in him,
　　because we trust in his holy name.
Let your steadfast love, O Lord, be upon us,
　　even as we hope in you.

Gospel
Luke 17:11–19

All　　　　Praise to you, Lord Jesus Christ.

Faith Reflection
Paul tells us that we should offer ourselves as sacrifices to God. Our lives should be an offering to God just as Jesus' life was an offering. In offering up our sickness and suffering, we share in the suffering of Jesus on the cross. It is only through accepting our suffering willingly, as Jesus did, that we will inherit eternal life. (*A personal witness on the power of prayer and God's healing touch may be appropriate.*)

Ritual Action
(*Conduct an anointing of the sick, either sacramental or a simple anointing as a reminder that all of us need to be healed.*)

Intercessions
Response: Lord, we ask you to heal us.

For those suffering from physical sickness . . .
For those suffering from mental sickness . . .
For those suffering from emotional sickness . . .
For those who are terminally ill . . .
For the families of those who are sick . . .
For doctors, nurses, and caregivers of the sick . . .
For acceptance of God's will in our lives . . .

Lord's Prayer

Blessing

Healing and loving God,
watch over those who are suffering from sickness or disease.
Give them, their families, and those who care for them
the strength they need to accept your will in their lives.
May all we do in your name
serve our brothers and sisters
until we enjoy our eternal reward
in the kingdom you have prepared for us.
This we ask through Christ our Lord.

All   Amen.

Closing Song

(See suggested songs in the Appendix.)

One Step at a Time

Focus

To ask God's help for all people addicted to drugs or alcohol, and to give strength to those who are addicted or recovering

(Be sure that all assignments have been made and that all required materials are on hand.)

Opening Song

(See suggested songs in the Appendix.)

Prayer

Healing Lord,
you command us to love freely
and to love one another as ourselves.
By our prayer, may we and all people
be free from addiction
and remain free from drug and alcohol abuse.
We pray this through Christ our Lord.

All   Amen.

Dramatic Reading

Acts 9:1–19

(The narrator text in parentheses may be omitted.)

Narrator   (Meanwhile) Saul, still breathing threats and murder against the disciples of the Lord, went to the high priest and asked him for letters to the synagogues at Damascus, so that if he found any who belonged to the Way, men or women, he might bring them bound to Jerusalem. Now as he was going along and approaching Damascus, suddenly a light from heaven flashed around him. He fell to the ground and heard a voice (saying to him)

Jesus   Saul, Saul, why do you persecute me?

Saul   (He asked) Who are you, Lord?

Jesus   (The reply came) I am Jesus, whom you are persecuting. But get up and enter the city, and you will be told what you are to do.

Narrator   The men who were traveling with him stood speechless because they heard the voice but saw no one. Saul got up from the ground and though his eyes were open, he could see nothing; so they led him by the hand and brought him into Damascus. For three days he was without sight, and neither ate nor drank. Now there was a disciple in Damascus named Ananias. The Lord said to him in a vision,

Jesus   Ananias.

Ananias   (He answered) Here I am, Lord.

Jesus   (The Lord said to him) Get up and go to the street called Straight, and at the house of Judas look for a man of Tarsus named Saul. At this moment he is praying, and he has seen in a vision a man named Ananias come in and lay his hands on him so that he might regain his sight.

Ananias   (But Ananias answered the Lord) Lord, I have heard from many about this man, how much evil he has done to your saints in Jerusalem; and here he has authority from the chief priests to bind all who invoke your name.

Jesus   (But the Lord said to him) Go, for he is an instrument I have chosen to bring my name before Gentiles and kings and before the people Israel; I myself will show him how much he must suffer for the sake of my name.

Narrator   So Ananias went and entered the house. He laid his hands on Saul (and said)

Ananias   Brother Saul, the Lord Jesus, who appeared to you on your way here, has sent me so that you may regain your sight and be filled with the Holy Spirit.

Narrator   And immediately something like scales fell from his eyes, and his sight was restored. Then he got up and was baptized, and after taking some food, he regained his strength. The word of the Lord.

All   Thanks be to God.

Responsorial
Psalm 25 "To You, O Lord" (Haugen)
or Psalm 121:

Response: My help comes from the Lord.

I lift up my eyes to the hills
    from where will my help come?
My help comes from the Lord,
    who made heaven and earth.

He will not let your foot be moved;
 he who keeps you will not slumber.
He who keeps Israel
 will neither slumber nor sleep.

The Lord is your keeper;
 the Lord is your shade at your right hand.
The sun shall not strike you by day,
 nor the moon by night.

The Lord will keep you from all evil;
 he will keep your life.
The Lord will keep your going out and your coming in
 from this time on and forevermore.

Gospel
Luke 5:17–26

All   Praise to you, Lord Jesus Christ.

Faith Reflection
Saul was converted by a devastating experience to being a follower of Jesus; so too is there great power and healing for those who go through the traumatic process of addiction recovery. Jesus has the power through our relationship with him and with his church to heal us and keep us spiritually healthy. *(A recovering addict or alcoholic's story of conversion may be very effective and should always include the importance of faith in the healing process.)*

Ritual Action
(Invite those gathered to sign a pledge against the use of alcohol or drugs. Collect the pledges and present them to all gathered in a basket held high as the following is said by one or all:)

Lord, you alone know our heart's desire. As we have pledged our faith and trust in you by signing this pledge to abstain from the use of alcohol or drugs, we ask you to strengthen and guide us in your love by loving our neighbor as ourselves. Accept these signed pledges as a sign of our faith in you and your power to overcome our human frailties. God, grant me the serenity to change the things I can, accept what I cannot change and come to know the difference.

Intercessions
Response: Lord, strengthen us.

When we are troubled or confused . . .
When we are lonely or feeling abandoned . . .

When we long for something greater than we long for you . . .
When our families are torn by alcohol or drugs . . .
When one among us falls to the temptation of drugs or alcohol . . .
When we are called to support each other . . .

Lord's Prayer

Blessing

Loving and merciful God,
heal those who suffer from any addiction.
Strengthen their families.
Increase in us the faith we need
to stay free from all addictions.
We call on you to heal the addicted.
This we ask through Christ our Lord.

All   Amen.

Closing Song

(See suggested songs in the Appendix.)

God's Family
Ethnic Appreciation

Focus
To appreciate being created in God's image and the blessing of human diversity

(Be sure that all assignments have been made and that all required materials are on hand.)

Opening Song
(See suggested songs in the Appendix.)

Prayer
God of all peoples,
you made us in your divine image
to emphasize that we are all your children.
Allow the colors and languages of humanity
to enrich creation as you planned.
May they reveal the diversity
with which you blessed us from the dawn of creation.
Through our prayer today,
may we appreciate the unity and diversity
of all our brothers and sisters in the world.
We make this prayer in your glorious name.

All   Amen.

Reading
Genesis 1:26–31

All   Thanks be to God.

Responsorial
Psalm 98 "All the Ends of the Earth" (Haas/Haugen)
or Psalm 148:

Response: Praise the Lord! Praise the Lord from the heavens; praise God in the heights!

Praise him, all his angels; praise him, all his host!
 Praise him, sun and moon; praise him, all you shining stars!
Praise him, you highest heavens,
  and you waters above the heavens!

Let them praise the name of the Lord,
    for he commanded and they were created.
He established them forever and ever;
    he fixed their bounds, which cannot be passed.

Praise the Lord from the earth,
    you sea monsters and all deeps,
fire and hail, snow and frost,
    stormy wind fulfilling his command!

Mountains and all hills, fruit trees and all cedars!
    Wild animals and all cattle, creeping things and flying birds!
Kings of the earth and all peoples, princes, all rulers of the earth!
    Young men and women alike, old and young together.

Let them praise the name of the Lord, for his name alone is exalted;
    his glory is above earth and heaven.
He has raised up a horn for his people, praise for all his faithful,
    for the people of Israel who are close to him.
Praise the Lord!

Gospel
Matthew 5:1–12

All   Praise to you, Lord Jesus Christ.

Faith Reflection
Human beings are all created in the divine image, but too often we think only of those characteristics that separate us from one another. Rather, we should recognize and celebrate what unites us as members of one human family. The beatitudes guide us in how we should treat one another as brothers and sisters. There is more that unites us than separates us.

Ritual Action
(While someone sings or plays "Abba Father," pass a bowl of water around the group allowing each person to sign the cross on the forehead of the person next to them.)

Intercessions
Response: Lord, unite us in your divine image.

When we see someone with a skin color different than ours . . .
When we hear someone speak a language different than ours . . .
When we see an ethnic custom different than ours . . .
When we taste an ethnic food different than what we are used to . . .
When we recognize differences between us and others . . .

Lord's Prayer

Blessing
Holy God, one and three,
may we always praise you
for making us in your image
and realize the blessing of diversity in your creation.
Strengthen and guide us
to treat each person as a blessing of your human family.
This we ask through Christ our Lord.

All   Amen.

Closing Song
(See suggested songs in the Appendix.)

Celebrating Family

Focus

To thank God for our family and all families and to ask for strength and perseverance when it is difficult to be a part of a family

(Be sure that all assignments have been made and that all required materials are on hand.)

Opening Song

(See suggested songs in the Appendix.)

Prayer

O God, more than father and mother to us,
as Jesus was a member of the holy family,
so we gather to thank you for our holy families:
parents, sisters, brothers, and relatives,
and to ask you for the perseverance and strength
to remain pleasing in your sight
when difficult times arise within our families.
We make this prayer according to your will.

All   Amen.

Reading

Ephesians 6:1–4

All   Thanks be to God.

Responsorial

Psalm 95 "If Today You Hear His Voice" (Haas)
or Psalm 121:

Response: My help comes from the Lord, who made heaven and earth.

I lift up my eyes to the hills
    from where will my help come?
My help comes from the Lord,
    who made heaven and earth.

He will not let your foot be moved;
    he who keeps you will not slumber.
He who keeps Israel
    will neither slumber nor sleep.

The Lord is your keeper;
    the Lord is your shade at your right hand.
The sun shall not strike you by day,
    nor the moon by night.

The Lord will keep you from all evil;
    he will keep your life.
The Lord will keep your going out and your coming in
    from this time on and forevermore.

Gospel
Luke 2:41–52

All   Praise to you, Lord Jesus Christ.

Faith Reflection
Paul teaches that children should obey their parents and that parents should by their example be good teachers to their children. Joseph and Mary are shaken by losing their son in the temple, but Jesus later obeys them and returns home with them. The example of Jesus should be a guide to teenagers as they strive to live in peace with their parents, brothers, and sisters. Though obedience to parents is difficult, it is necessary for peace and stability in a home.

Ritual Action
(Family members take turns standing in the middle of their family formed in a circle. Family members in the circle place their hand on the family member in the middle as a sign of prayer and support. Reflective music might be played during this ritual.)

Intercessions
Response: Loving God, help us.

For all families, especially those affected by sickness, divorce, separation
    or death . . .
For all who suffer abuse in their families . . .
For all who have a difficult home life . . .
For respect of all life . . .
For love in our families . . .
For our extended families and our friends . . .

Lord's Prayer

Blessing

Merciful and loving God,
as you blessed Joseph, Mary, and Jesus as the holy family,
so too bless our families to be faithful and loving.
May we be respectful toward one another
and treat each family member as we would treat Jesus.
This we ask through Christ our Lord.

All   Amen.

Closing Song

(See suggested songs in the Appendix.)

Celebrating Freedom

Focus

To show appreciation for the gift of freedom, from death and sin, from oppression and want

(Be sure that all assignments have been made and that all required materials are on hand.)

Opening Song

(See suggested songs in the Appendix.)

Prayer

God of freedom and justice,
we thank you for the courage of our ancestors
to live and die for our freedom.
May our work and prayer strengthen us
to work for the freedom of all.
We ask this through Jesus Christ our savior.

All   Amen.

Reading

Romans 6:1–14

All   Thanks be to God.

Responsorial

Psalm 104 "Lord, Send Out Your Spirit" (Haas)
or Psalm 67:

Response: God, our God, has blessed us.

May God be gracious to us and bless us
    and make his face to shine upon us.
that your way may be known upon earth,
    your saving power among all nations.

Let the peoples praise you, O God;
    let all the peoples praise you.
Let the nations be glad and sing for joy,
    for you judge the peoples with equity
    and guide the nations upon earth.
Let the peoples praise you, O God;
    let all the peoples praise you.

The earth has yielded its increase;
God, our God, has blessed us.

Gospel
John 8:31–38

All Praise to you, Lord Jesus Christ.

Faith Reflection
Paul teaches that Christ offered us the greatest freedom of all: freedom from sin. Our own sinfulness often enslaves us. By his death and resurrection, Jesus won for us freedom from sin and death. Our life should be focused on freeing others from what enslaves them: sickness, abuse, racism, sexism . . .

Ritual Action
(Youths write down how they would complete the sentence, "I am thankful to be free to . . ." The papers are collected and read to the group. Another option would be for the youths to write down their answers to the same questions on a large piece of cardboard and then decorate it with symbols of freedom.)

Intercessions
Response: Thank you, O Lord.

For freeing us from sin and death . . .
For the perseverance of our ancestors . . .
For the faith and witness of the martyrs . . .
For the love of those who protect us in our armed forces . . .
For the strength you give us to help free others . . .

Lord's Prayer

Blessing
Faithful and freeing God,
may we never forget what you have done for us
through the death and resurrection of your son, Jesus.
Strengthen us to help all peoples
be free from injustice and oppression.
May we always work for the freedom of all people.
This we ask through Christ our Lord.

All Amen.

Closing Song
(See suggested songs in the Appendix.)

One in Christ

Focus
To promote unity among members of various groups that feel a need to disassociate themselves from each other

(Be sure that all assignments have been made and that all required materials are on hand.)

Opening Song
(See suggested songs in the Appendix.)

Prayer
Merciful and loving God,
you call us to love others
as you love us,
to accept others as your sons and daughters.
Help us to promote the good works
of justice, peace, and love.
May our prayer today knock down
the barriers that divide us
and instead unite us to overcome injustice of any kind.
We ask this in the name of you, the God of peace.

All   Amen.

Reading
Galatians 4:8–15

All   Thanks be to God.

Responsorial
"Prayer of St. Francis" (Temple)
or Psalm 86:

Response: You are my God; be gracious to me, O Lord.

Incline your ear, O Lord, and answer me,
  for I am poor and needy.
Preserve my life, for I am devoted to you;
  save your servant who trusts in you.

You are my God; be gracious to me, O Lord,
  for to you do I cry all day long.
Gladden the soul of your servant,

for to you, O Lord, I lift up my soul.

For you, O Lord, are good and forgiving,
   abounding in steadfast love to all who call on you.
Give ear, O Lord, to my prayer;
   listen to my cry of supplication.

In the day of my trouble I call on you,
   for you will answer me.
There is none like you among the gods, O Lord,
   nor are there any works like yours.

All the nations you have made shall come
   and bow down before you, O Lord.
   and shall glorify your name.
For you are great and do wondrous things;
   you alone are God.

Teach me your way, O Lord,
   that I may walk in your truth;
   give me an undivided heart to revere your name.
I give thanks to you, O Lord my God, with my whole heart,
   and I will glorify your name forever.
For great is your steadfast love toward me;
   you have delivered my soul
   from the depths of Sheol.

O God, the insolent rise up against me;
   a band of ruffians seeks my life,
   and they do not set you before them.
But you, O Lord, are a God merciful and gracious,
   slow to anger and abounding in steadfast love and faithfulness.

Gospel
Matthew 18:19–35

All   Praise to you, Lord Jesus Christ.

Faith Reflection
Paul challenges us to act like Christ by carrying the burdens of others. When we care for, console, or empathize with another, we help them to carry the burdens that weigh them down. By our prayer with others, Christ is present in our gathering. Gangs or cliques don't usually gather for positive, life-giving purposes. Members of gangs or cliques might not see the need to be members if they were offered something positive and helpful.

Ritual Action

(Youths write down on a piece of paper something that makes them similar to everyone else and something that makes them different from everyone else. The papers are lit from a candle near a metal can and placed in the metal can. Incense may also be added to the fire. After the papers are burned, each youth is signed with a cross on the forehead from the ashes. This ritual impresses upon the youths that each of us must respect the differences and similarities among us.)

Intercessions

Response: Lord, unite us in your love.

When we forget that you made us in your divine image . . .
When we sin against your commandments . . .
When we show disrespect to you or others . . .
When we show hatred toward someone . . .
When we injure another by word or action . . .
When we make fun of others . . .

Lord's Prayer

Blessing

Faithful and loving God,
your son Jesus showed the disciples how to love,
serve each other, and put differences aside.
Guide us to show respect and appreciation
for the people you have placed in our lives.
May we be always ready to forgive and be forgiven.
Help us to remember that when we gather
you are in our midst.
This we ask through Christ our Lord.

All   Amen.

Closing Song

(See suggested songs in the Appendix.)

Preferential Option

Focus
To ask God's help to be faithful ministers to those who are poor

(Be sure that all assignments have been made and that all required materials are on hand.)

Opening Song
(See suggested songs in the Appendix.)

Prayer
God of all-embracing love,
as Jesus ministered and preached to all people,
may our prayer today help us realize
that when we serve those
who are needy or poor, we are serving Christ.
We make this prayer in our Savior's name.

All   Amen.

Reading
Acts 4:32–35

All   Thanks be to God.

Responsorial
Psalm 95 "If Today You Hear His Voice" (Haas)
or Psalm 34:

Response:
I will bless the Lord at all times; God's praise shall continually be in my mouth.

My soul makes its boast in the Lord;
   let the humble hear and be glad.
O magnify the Lord with me,
   and let us exalt his name together.

I sought the Lord, and he answered me,
   and delivered me from all my fears.
Look to him, and be radiant;
   so your faces shall never be ashamed.

This poor soul cried, and was heard by the Lord,

and was saved from every trouble.
The angel of the Lord encamps around those who fear him,
   and delivers them.

O taste and see that the Lord is good;
   happy are those who take refuge in him.
O fear the Lord, you his holy ones,
   for those who fear him have no want.

Gospel
Matthew 25:31–40

All   Praise to you, Lord Jesus Christ.

Faith Reflection
Our greatest gift is our faith, not positions of authority or our possessions. We express and share our faith by assisting others with food, clothing, housing, or other means of assistance. Our faith and our daily acts of love feed upon each other. Serving our neighbor is not an extra responsibility of the followers of Jesus, but an integral part of living out the gospel. Though our efforts may seem useless when matched against the needs of our neighborhood and the world, our assistance to others reveals the love that God has for the poor.

Ritual Action
(There should be a procession with food and other offerings for the poor. Those who are going to work in a soup kitchen or social service place might be part of the procession. The ritual might be the work they do, while the prayer would be at the beginning and end of their work.)

Intercessions
Response: Help us, Lord, to serve those in need.

When people suffer from poverty and hunger . . .
When people are homeless . . .
When people are strangers in a foreign land . . .
When people are orphaned or widowed . . .
When people are rejected for their race . . .
When people are scorned for their ethnic background . . .
When people are made fun of for their religion . . .
When people are in need . . .

Lord's Prayer

Blessing

Lord, as you taught us by the life and death of Jesus,
strengthen us to help all people who are in need.
May our faith guide us to serve the least ones
as we would serve Christ.
This we ask through Christ our Lord.

All   Amen.

Closing Song

(See suggested songs in the Appendix.)

Praying Always

Focus

To remind ourselves of the importance of prayer, which should be an integral part of the Christian life

(Be sure that all assignments have been made and that all required materials are on hand.)

Opening Song

(See suggested songs in the Appendix.)

Prayer

Eternal and faithful God,
Jesus taught his disciples to pray
intimately and personally—to call you Abba.
Through our prayer today,
may we acknowledge that we were made to love freely
and that all we do is our prayer to you.
We make this prayer in Jesus' name.

All   Amen.

Reading

Ephesians 6:10–20

All   Thanks be to God.

Responsorial

Psalm 100 "We Are His People" (Haas)
or Psalm 5:

Response: Listen to the sound of my cry, my king and my God.

Give ear to my words, O Lord;
    give heed to my sighing.
Listen to the sound of my cry,
    my King and my God, for to you I pray.
O Lord, in the morning you hear my voice;
    in the morning I plead my case to you, and watch.

For you are not a God who delights in the wickedness;
    evil will not sojourn with you.
The boastful will not stand before your eyes;
    you hate all evildoers.

You destroy those who speak lies;
    the Lord abhors the bloodthirsty and deceitful.

But I, through the abundance of your steadfast love,
    will enter your house,
I will bow down toward your holy temple in awe of you.
Lead me, O Lord, in your righteousness because of my enemies;
    make your way straight before me.

But let all who take refuge in you rejoice;
    let them ever sing for joy.
Spread your protection over them,
    so that those who love your name may exult in you.
For you bless the righteous, O Lord;
    you cover them with favor as with a shield.

Gospel
Matthew 6:5–15

All   Praise to you, Lord Jesus Christ.

Faith Reflection
Paul constantly exhorted his readers to pray for one another. Jesus taught his disciples how to pray; he taught them to pray for and to forgive one another. Prayer should focus on finding and then doing God's will. We should be more intent on praying "for" someone, rather than "that" something will or won't happen. Our prayer, joined with that of others, can help us follow in the footsteps of Jesus.

Ritual Action
(In darkness, a large candle is placed in the middle of all gathered in a circle. Each person has an unlit taper. One by one each person stands up and prays [out loud is preferred] and then proceeds to light their taper from the Christ candle in the center to symbolize an answer to the prayer. When all candles are lit, invite all to stand, hold their tapers in their left hands, and put their right hand on the right shoulder of the person to their right. Proceed with the Lord's Prayer.)

Lord's Prayer

Blessing

Almighty God, you taught us to call on you in prayer.
Increase our awareness of your invitation
to ask for what we need,
to approach you with confidence,

to pray with humble gratitude.
May we always be more concerned
with accepting your will for us
than with trying to force our will on you.
This we ask through Christ our Lord.

All   Amen.

Closing Song

(See suggested songs in the Appendix.)

Called in Christ

Focus
To pray for openness to God's call to do his will in our lives

(Be sure that all assignments have been made and that all required materials are on hand.)

Opening Song
(See suggested songs in the Appendix.)

Prayer
Holy and righteous God,
as Jesus called his disciples
to work close to him in his ministry,
you call us by our baptism
to minister to the people you have placed in our lives.
May our prayer keep our minds and hearts
open to the ways we can serve
as ministers of your holy will.
We ask this through Christ, your servant and our savior.

All	Amen.

Dramatic Reading
1 Samuel 3:1–21
(The narrator text in parentheses may be omitted.)

Narrator	Now the boy Samuel was ministering to the Lord under Eli. The word of the Lord was rare in those days; visions were not widespread. At that time Eli, whose eyesight had begun to grow dim so that he could not see, was lying down in his room; the lamp of God had not yet gone out, and Samuel was lying down in the temple of the Lord, where the ark of God was. Then the Lord called
Lord	Samuel! Samuel!
Narrator	(and he said)
Samuel	Here I am!
Narrator	and ran to Eli (and said)
Samuel	Here I am, for you called me.

Narrator	But he said
Eli	I did not call; lie down again.
Narrator	So he went and lay down. The Lord called again
Lord	Samuel!
Narrator	Samuel got up and went to Eli, (and said)
Samuel	Here I am, for you called me.
Narrator	(But he said)
Eli	I did not call, my son; lie down again.
Narrator	Now Samuel did not yet know the Lord, and the word of the Lord had not yet been revealed to him. The Lord called Samuel again, a third time. And he got up and went to Eli, (and said)
Samuel	Here I am, for you called me.
Narrator	Then Eli perceived that the Lord was calling the boy. (Therefore Eli said to Samuel)
Eli	Go lie down and if he calls you, you shall say, "Speak, Lord, for your servant is listening."
Narrator	So Samuel went and lay down in his place. Now the Lord came and stood there, (calling as before)
Lord	Samuel! Samuel!
Narrator	(And Samuel said)
Samuel	Speak, for your servant is listening.
Narrator	(Then the Lord said to Samuel)
Lord	See I am about to do something in Israel that will make both ears of anyone who hears of it tingle. On that day I will fulfill against Eli all that I have spoken concerning his house, from beginning to end. For I have told him that I am about to punish his house forever, for the iniquity that he knew, because his sons were blaspheming God, and he did not restrain them. Therefore I swear to the house of Eli that the iniquity of Eli's house shall not be expiated by sacrifice or offering forever.

Narrator	Samuel lay there until morning; then he opened the doors of the house of the Lord. Samuel was afraid to tell the vision to Eli. But Eli called Samuel (and said)
Eli	Samuel, my son.
Narrator	(He said)
Samuel	Here I am.
Narrator	(Eli said)
Eli	What was it that he told you? Do not hide it from me, May God do so to you and more also, if you hide anything from me of all that he told you.
Narrator	So Samuel told him everything and hid nothing from him. (Then he said)
Eli	It is the Lord; let him do what seems good to him.
Narrator	As Samuel grew up, the Lord was with him and let none of his words fall to the ground. All Israel from Dan to Beersheba knew that Samuel was a trustworthy prophet of the Lord. The Lord continued to appear at Shiloh by the word of the Lord. And the word of Samuel came to all Israel. The word of the Lord.
All	Thanks be to God.
	or Jeremiah 1:4–10
All	Thanks be to God.

Responsorial
"The Lord Is My Light" (Haas)

Gospel
Luke 5:1–11

All	Praise to you, Lord Jesus Christ.

Faith Reflection
As Samuel and Jeremiah were called in unique ways to God's work, we too are uniquely called to it. Each of us is called to do God's work in whatever form that may be. All of us are called to union with God and with one another. All of us are called to be people of prayer. All of us are called to be of service to others. This may be achieved as a religious brother or sister, as a married person, as a single person—anyone following the Lord's call.

Ritual Action
(Invite all present to write down how they will serve as a witness to God's will. Collect the pieces of paper in a basket. Present the basket as all recite the Lord's Prayer.)

Lord's Prayer

Blessing
Loving God,
may we always imitate the disciples
and be your witnesses when you call us to your service.
Strengthen us always to be open
to your call in our lives.
Make us ready to accept the challenges of ministry.
This we ask through Christ our Lord.

All   Amen.

Closing Song
(See suggested songs in the Appendix.)

Appendix

Opening Songs

Blest Be the Lord - Schutte (Oregon Catholic Press, OCP)
Gather Us In - Haugen (Gregorian Institute of America, GIA)
Glory and Praise to Our God - Schutte (OCP)
Here I Am, Lord - Schutte (OCP)
I Am Yours Today - Haas (GIA)
Jesus, Come to Us - Haas (GIA)
Joyfully Singing - Dameans (GIA)
Lift Up Your Hearts - O'Connor (OCP)
Praise God from Whom All Blessings Flow - Traditional

Responsorials

(These may replace the suggested responsorial psalms if so desired.)
I Have Loved You - Joncas (OCP)
I Lift Up My Soul - Manion (OCP)
Remember Your Love - Dameans (GIA)
We Praise You - Dameans (GIA)

Closing Songs

Blest Are They - Haas (GIA)
City of God - Schutte (OCP)
Light of Christ - Kendzia (OCP)
Lover of Us All - Schutte (OCP)
Now Thank We All Our God - Traditional
Servant Song - Cooney (GIA)
Sing to the Mountains - Dufford (OCP)
Though the Mountains May Fall - Schutte (OCP)
What You Hear in the Dark - Schutte (OCP)

Comfort and Support

Be Not Afraid - Dufford (OCP)
Eye Has Not Seen - Haugen (GIA)
Healer of My Soul - Talbot
I Am the Bread of Life - Toolan (GIA)
I, the Lord - Kendzia (OCP)
Lay Your Hands - Landry (OCP)
On Eagle's Wings - Joncas (GIA)
You Are Near - Schutte (OCP)

Confirmation

Come, Holy Ghost - Traditional
Come, O Spirit of the Lord - Kendzia (OCP)
He Has Anointed Me - Dameans (GIA)
Send Us Your Spirit - Haas (GIA) or Schutte (OCP)

Family

Faithful Family - Cooney (GIA)
Nobody's Home - Boltz
We Are Many Parts - Haugen (GIA)

Lent

Behold, the Wood - Schutte (OCP)
Jesus, Remember Me - Taizé (GIA)
Jesus, the Lord - O'Connor (OCP)
My God, My God - Manion (OCP)
Pieta - Kendzia (OCP)
Were You There? - Traditional

Peace and Justice

Anthem - Conry (OCP)
Change Our Hearts - Cooney (GIA)
Cry of the Poor - Foley (OCP)
Living God - Haas (GIA)
Peace Prayer - Foley (OCP)
The Harvest of Justice - Haas (GIA)

To order music for any of the above songs, or to request reprint permissions, contact the publishers below:

Gregorian Institute of America (GIA)
7404 So. Mason Avenue
Chicago, IL 60638
1-708-496-3800

Oregon Catholic Press (OCP)
5536 NE Hassalo
Portland, OR 97213
1-800-548-8749

Of Related Interest...

Seasonal Prayer Services for Teenagers
Greg Dues
This collection of 16 prayer services helps teenagers understand the themes found in the holidays of the seasons, the church year and the civic year.
ISBN: 0-89622-473-2, 80 pp, $9.95

Teen Prayer Services
20 Themes for Reflection
Kevin Regan
This book is meant to help teenagers touch life in all its paradoxes by inviting them into a dialogue with God. Great for retreats, special sessions and regular classes.
ISBN: 0-89622-520-8, 80 pp, $9.95

20 More Teen Prayer Services
Kevin Regan
Each prayer service contains a mini-lesson, and includes suggested times for use, a list of materials needed, an introduction, shared experience and the prayer service.
ISBN: 0-89622-605-0, 112 pp, $9.95

Teen Assemblies, Retreats and Prayer Services
Greg Dues
Dues uses Scripture, reflection, discussion and activities to help teens explore the concepts and traditions of their faith.
ISBN: 0-89622-561-5, 96 pp, $9.95

Why Go To Mass
Reasons and Resources to Motivate Teenagers
Greg Dues
Each of the eight chapters in this book contains five to seven worksheets for teenagers, as well as background and introductory materials for teachers and parents.
ISBN: 0-89622-604-2, 72 pp, $9.95

Available at religious bookstores or from
TWENTY-THIRD PUBLICATIONS
P.O. Box 180 • Mystic, CT 06355
1-800-321-0411